Also by Brian Domitrovic

*Taxes Have Consequences: An Income
Tax History of the United States*

FREE MONEY

BITCOIN
and the
AMERICAN
Monetary Tradition

BRIAN DOMITROVIC
& BENTON HOWSER

A POST HILL PRESS BOOK
ISBN: 979-8-88845-976-8
ISBN (eBook): 979-8-88845-977-5

Free Money:
Bitcoin and the American Monetary Tradition
© 2025 by Brian Domitrovic and Benton Howser
All Rights Reserved

Cover design by Cody Corcoran

Post Hill Press
New York • Nashville
posthillpress.com

Published in the United States of America
1 2 3 4 5 6 7 8 9 10

CONTENTS

Foreword   by Dr. Arthur B. Laffer vii

Prologue   Time and Gold xi

Chapter 1   Introduction: A Monetary Collective
Unconscious 1

Chapter 2   The Industrial Revolution—In Money...............24

Chapter 3   The American Way of Currency.........................51

Chapter 4   Antebellum Alternatives: A United
States Bank or Free Banking...........................73

Chapter 5   Toward a Federal Takeover 96

Chapter 6   Here Comes the Fed 128

Chapter 7   The Reserve Currency Era I: Bretton Woods 151

Chapter 8   The Reserve Currency Era II: Bitcoin Arrives ...173

Conclusion: The World Ahead 193

Bibliographic Note and Acknowledgments..........................205

About the Authors...209

by Dr. Arthur B. Laffer

Before I ever was known as a tax economist, I was a currency economist. In the 1960s, as a graduate student at Stanford University and then ascending in the ranks at the University of Chicago, I studied, wrote, and published about what kind of money people the world over like to have. I was a "trade" economist, in the jargon of the field. I was interested in what monetary media people voluntarily take in exchange for the product of their labor and capital commitments. I found that, globally, people love to trade their own products for the money of the places that have exceptional growth potential. If a place is going to grow and prosper, you want to have whatever money works in that place. To invest in an area on the cusp of a boom—people will do anything to get the instrument, the money, that works in that place.

Events came crashing down. In 1971, while I was working for the administration (as the Chief Economist, under director George Shultz, of the Office of Management and Budget), President Nixon took the dollar off gold. All bets were off.

Exchange the product of your labor and capital commitments for fiat money? Fat chance. Before 1971, the dollar was convertible in gold at a fixed price ($35 per ounce), and other currencies were convertible to the dollar (and by extension, gold), at fixed rates of exchange. After 1971, who knew what any currency was worth.

I fought this transition as it happened, valiantly I do believe, but it came nonetheless. And then people said forget it, I'll decline to produce and instead dedicate myself to protecting my assets. On came the 1970s. The decade of stagflation—recession plus inflation—had everyone scrambling into gold, silver, art, durables, land, anything that could get them out of currencies.

"Stagflation" in the 1970s forced me to become a tax economist. If someone were to lower their marginal rate of taxation—thus increasing the after-tax return on labor and capital—money would flow there, and out of the myriad hedges, I reasoned. At last, beginning in 1978, the United States started to cut its tax rates. It took the capital gains tax rate down from an unconscionable 50 percent (unadjusted for inflation) to a we-can-talk 28 percent. California cut its property tax by 60 percent and capped future increases. When Ronald Reagan became president in 1981, he made it his purpose to cut tax rates over and over. The top rate of the income tax, under Reagan, plummeted from 70 to 28 percent. As all this took hold, people decided that they wanted the dollar again, and big time. The dollar price of gold and of foreign exchange fell like a stone. Economic growth did the opposite. It took off like a rocket.

Reagan proved that fiat money can work—if you lower tax rates, in particular at the top. People raced to get the dollar in the 1980s and the 1990s, as the economy explored new heights of prosperity. In the new millennium, once again people wanted the dollar not so much—as the federal government opted for spending, spending, spending, over further marginal tax cuts (a wonderful exception was the Tax Cuts and Jobs Act of 2017).

I am going into all this because over my long career, it has become clear to me (not that I didn't know it at the outset), the public detests fiat money and loves, loves, loves classical money, above all money convertible in gold. The fiat dollar can work, if tax rates are competitively very low. Otherwise, people want hard money, classical money, gold and silver money, like for eons in the past.

Bitcoin has occasionally been worth, in total in the markets, $2 trillion. That's something. Lots of people with lots of money have devoted their resources to this development. We should listen to them. Bitcoin is private money, and as this book so resoundingly details, private money has been our history up to quite recently, within my own professional lifetime. People love private money, far and away more than the feelings they have for government fiat money, and they have good reason to love it. It was the money that accompanied the economy to its greatest heights in years past, before our eras of stagflation and "secular stagnation."

We used to have a gold standard—and we did so well while having it. The price level was stable for over a century before the founding of the Fed in 1913, while the money supply, along with economic growth, expanded like crazy. We had a price rule for our money. A dollar was explicitly worth something—a twentieth of an ounce of gold. Since the Fed was founded, the dollar has collapsed in value by 98 percent—huh? Why did we ever abandon classical money?

I can perfectly see a future in which Americans seek to reclaim their monetary legacy and redefine the dollar in a foundational asset. Gold served in times past, and now here is Bitcoin.

The idea that the fiat Fed dollar is going to be our be-all-and-end-all currency for the next hundred years is fanciful. Of course we are going to have monetary innovation, and if we do it right, for the better. Bitcoin is a fascinating, hugely popular, and technically masterful response to our currency crisis. Think it's not in accord with our glorious history? Read *Free Money*.

PROLOGUE

Time and Gold

This book has two purposes. The first is to show what money is and how issuers of money used to work. The second is to show that the new blockchain technology (represented predominantly by Bitcoin) has the capacity to bring into the present day the principles of good, sound money of a glorious past of economic growth and prosperity. The future promises to be no less flourishing.

In his domain (in modern-day Peru) in 1532, the Inca king Atahuallpa marched with several thousand lightly armed attendants into a courtyard where a small force of armed-to-the-teeth Spaniards massacred everyone except him. (It was similar to the Red Wedding, except for the king-living part.) Atahuallpa proposed to his captors that he ransom himself. As William Prescott recounted the episode in his *History of the Conquest of Peru* (1847), Atahuallpa "would engage to cover the floor of the apartment on which they stood with gold…. He said, with some emphasis, that 'he would not merely cover the floor, but would fill the room with gold as high as he could reach'; and, standing on tiptoe, he stretched out his hand against the wall." Atahuallpa's captor Francisco Pizarro set to "drawing a red line along the wall at the height which the Inca had indicated. The apartment was about seventeen feet broad, by twenty-two feet long, and the line round the walls was nine feet from the floor."[1]

Over the course of several months, the room slowly filled, care of the deliveries of the king's further minions, until it topped out, in today's prices, with over $1 billion of gold. Two additional rooms were filled with silver (because why not?). Atahuallpa, however, did not live happily ever after. Pizarro still had him killed (as would have happened in *Game of Thrones*). The Spanish forces wanted all that gold and silver—not because it had value like oil would have in fueling a ship, or a large grain harvest would have in feeding livestock, but because gold and silver functioned exceptionally well as a store of value and a medium of exchange. When the Spanish hoarded the precious metals, they knew they were holding on to things that kept their value and would be worth that value when, with the metals, they sought to buy goods and services or to make an investment. Better than any other article over so many times and places in world history, gold and silver have had the central characteristics of money. Gold makes fine jewelry and has some manufacturing uses, but if it had greater value in those areas, most of it would not be kept in vaults.

The classical gold standard of the past was a system in which the paper money and bank loans that various entities and institutions issued had a definition in gold. This is different from only issuing gold coins. Money defined in gold (or gold and silver together) can expand and contract in supply according to

---

[1] William Hickling Prescott, *History of the Conquest of Peru* (Project Gutenberg, 2014), Ch. 5.

the requirements of the economy. The standard three-part definition of money is that money is 1) a medium of exchange or a transaction instrument, 2) a unit of account, and 3) a store of value. Money is a medium of exchange in that it is how people agree to get a deal done, exchanging goods and services, without bartering. Instead of swapping a tire for some milk, we use money to pay for the milk, and the milkman can go spend that money at a bar or wherever. Money is a unit of account in that it is a common metric by which things of different natures can be assessed against each other. Money is a store of value in that it retains (or should retain) its value through long durations, through even the ups and downs of eras and civilizations.

A unique aspect of gold is that it takes a certain amount of time to acquire new gold. The amount of gold extant is hard to increase, or for that matter, decrease (we have most of the gold ever mined in our possession today). Gold lies in the earth, usually deep, and mining takes time and lots of effort—lots of money—to get more of it. If we have to get more of it, it is a pain. Same with slightly more abundant silver. Therefore, societies have developed other forms of money—currency, bank loans—that take far less time to produce but are redeemable in gold or silver.

Judas betrayed Jesus for thirty pieces of silver. Thirty pieces of silver as of 2023 were worth about $700. That $700 was worth six months' income for a family two thousand years ago. Nowadays, $700 is less than a week's salary for the average family, or half a COVID check from Uncle Sam. Many tasks in the economy take less time now than ten years ago, one hundred years ago, or five hundred years ago. If it takes half a year's worth of labor to feed a person, then half the population has to work full time at farming. Less than 2 percent of the population are farmers now. (How many people get paid by the government not to farm?) Most people are no longer farmers because it no longer takes so much of everyone's time to get the food we eat. We use trackers and a whole array of new technologies and techniques instead of the plows and draft animals of the past. This has increased farm yields spectacularly. As for distribution, how many New Yorkers ate avocados regularly in 1776? A vacuum cleaner today costs the same in terms of work as it did in the 1950s. But vacuum cleaners today are lighter and sweep better than the iron-belled behemoths of yesteryear.

Properly functioning economies get more efficient. This means one thing above all: people are getting more efficient with their time. It is hard to believe that people these days who binge-watch an entire television show are efficient. But true enough, we are amazingly efficient compared to people in the past. Surely, we are no better than people in the past. We just have tools that they did not. Do you want to talk to someone ten miles away? Easy—pick up the phone and call the person. Better yet, just text. Almost all of our daily tasks take a fraction of the time that they used to. For fun, look up the cost required to light up a house before the light bulb or even Standard Oil.[2]

Gold and silver remain hard to get from the ground. Yet our use of time in making each thing of economic value has increased and increased. To spend time digging up gold and silver for money would appear to be a remarkable waste, because our time these days is so good, so effective, when applied to producing things. Yet the price of gold rose sevenfold (and silver

---

[2]   See William D. Nordhaus, "Do Real-Output and Real-Wage Measures Capture Reality? The History of Lighting Suggests Not," in *The Economics of New Goods*, eds. Timothy F. Bresnahan and Robert J. Gordon (Chicago: University of Chicago Press, 1996).

fivefold) in the first two decades of the 2000s, having been largely stable for ages. We have wasted time going after final money—gold and silver—because our nominal money, our dollars typically, have not held their value. The chief problem is that these dollars no longer abide by a definition in something very hard to get, like gold or silver, the great bases of money in the past.

If we get better at using our time, but our money devalues simultaneously, it is no different from extending the units of time while keeping our money constant. Extending units of time— saying one second is two seconds, for example—is ridiculous. We have to sleep eight of every twenty-four hours no matter how we wish to define a day. Given that we can measure value in terms of time efficiency against an unchanging unit of time, we should be able to measure value in terms of an unchanging unit of money. How much does thirty pieces of silver buy today compared to Year 33? Much more, in terms of both the price of stuff and its quantity, because of time efficiency.

Inflation and currency devaluation at even a moderate rate can lead to a loss of faith such that money loses its value and imperils people's entire savings, savings that can be lost even in short time spans. In the classical gold and silver standard eras, there was a constant feedback loop to those institutions, banks mainly, issuing money. If the issuers did not maintain the confidence of their depositors, there would be a bank run. A bank's job was to make as much money as possible without jeopardizing the confidence of their depositors. The level of confidence of the depositors was clear, measured by how much they did or did not demand that their money be redeemed in the base unit, gold or silver. Under a government-controlled fiat system, that duty was transferred to central banks. But nobody has deposits at the central banks outside of the banks themselves. And then the central banks said that they did not want to define their money in gold or silver anymore. Money devalued like nobody's business, even though the economy, for better or worse, generally stayed quite productive. What a world. Bitcoin beckons toward a new one.

If there is anything to remember from these pages, it is that first, prosperity and opportunity were the norm under classical, largely privately made money. The second is that all major crises in the world today connect in some manner to the store-of-value crisis. This crisis has been continuing, as of the 2020s, for 110 years, from the European powers' going off the gold standard during World War I, to the tenuous gold standard restoration of Bretton Woods after World War II, and finally to the gold window's closing in 1971, complete with the general ceding of monetary wisdom and authority to credentialed professionals (such as at the Federal Reserve). Money is broken because the store-of-value component—the most important part—is broken. When people say time is money, this is because money represents time stored. Stored time with modern money melts away like ice does in a drink.

CHAPTER 1

Introduction: A Monetary Collective Unconscious

In the 1984 movie *Revenge of the Nerds*, the heroes have a statement to make as the story comes to its conclusion. After a group of big-man-on-campus fraternity men trash the nerds' house at Adams College, the bespectacled Gilbert has this to say:

> I just wanted to say that I'm a nerd, and I'm here tonight to stand up for the rights of other nerds. I mean, all our lives we've been laughed at and made to feel inferior. And tonight, those bastards, they trashed our house. Why? Cause we're smart? Cause we look different? Well, we're not. I'm a nerd, and I'm pretty proud of it.

His friend Lewis comments as well:

> Hi, Gilbert. I'm a nerd too. I just found that out tonight. We have news for the beautiful

people. There's a lot more of us than there are of you. I know there's alumni here tonight. When you went to Adams you might've been called a spazz, or a dork, or a geek. Any of you that have ever felt stepped on, left out, picked on, put down, whether you think you're a nerd or not, why don't you just come down here and join us. Okay? Come on.

And then Gilbert again: "Just join us, cause no one's gonna really be free until nerd persecution ends." Before the speeches, Lewis had stolen the girlfriend of the quarterback of the football team.[3]

Three years later, in 1987, Microsoft founder William H. Gates became a billionaire. He was a "Bill-ionaire," as the *Economist* put it, next to a chart marking his stock's take-off. In the 1990s, mind-numbing fortune after mind-numbing fortune was made by the likes of Harvard dropout Gates, high-school valedictorian Jeff Bezos (founder of Amazon.com), and Trekkie-type Steve Wozniak (cofounder of Apple Computer). As the internet came into widespread use in that decade, innumerable aspects of business and daily life began to experience transformation. By the close of the millennium, the idiom "brick-and-mortar" had become current to describe the kind of establishments—those that sell their wares to customers in buildings such as shopping malls—that probably would bite the dust as the tech revolution fully unfolded in the twenty-first century. Among the first retrospectives of the remarkable

---

3   *Revenge of the Nerds* (1984), Anthony Edwards: Gilbert, at www.imdb.com/title/tt0088000/characters/nm0000381.

information technology revolution was the 1996 documentary titled *Triumph of the Nerds*.[4]

Today, it is rather unheard-of for a young person—a high school or college student, for example—to be ridiculed for being a computer junkie. It is assumed, in the 2020s, that if a young person has a natural interest and facility in internet architecture, virtual reality, artificial intelligence, gaming, websites, or streaming video, this person may, at the minimum, soon end up as a desired and well compensated professional. There is a non-negligible chance that this person will do more, such as become fatly rich and, in some noteworthy way, change the way lives are lived. As investing plutocrat Stanley Druckenmiller has remarked of Bezos, he is a "serial monopolist" strangling such blue-chip businesses as International Business Machines. Today, people keep a gimlet eye on the young computer aficionado. This person has an odds-on chance of rocking our world.[5]

Decades ago, in the early 1980s, in the culture attested to in the movie with Gilbert and Lewis, a smugness still prevailed concerning "nerds." In the movie, even though one of them got the girl, the most the nerds were generally bidding for was a basic minimum of acceptance and affection. The nerdy alums were encouraged to come down and join the group in a show of support and coming-out. In 1984, at the movie's release, there was, as yet, no sense that an earthquake in economic and, indeed, social life was about to come at the hands of just this group of dear people. Now we assume that ever more waves of computer types of the Gates-Bezos-Wozniak and Elon Musk sort will rock our world and continue to do so in unimaginable

---

4   "Early Riser," *The Economist*, March 28, 1987, 83.

5   Antoine Gara, "Why Billionaire Trader Stan Druckenmiller Believes in Amazon and Not IBM," Forbes.com, Nov. 3, 2015.

ways, not all of them comfortable, for fully the rest of our natural lives.

A thought might be spared for the social prejudice that got shunted aside in this process. What happened to the animus, once flourishing, to mock nerds? It got the comeuppance of the ages, to be sure. Did it just give up and fade away? If such phenomena behave like pathogens, this prejudice went into abeyance, bided its time, and cruised for new objects, new hosts. Among all the various developments within the technological revolution since the 1990s, perhaps only one wound up on the receiving end of the old, battered, conquered-but-still-determined anti-nerd social prejudice. This was the development of cryptocurrency, specifically Bitcoin.

Bitcoin launched the cryptocurrency movement in October 2008. A publication of a pseudonymous white paper that month introduced Bitcoin, by name, as a new transferable but un-sharable and permanently publicly recorded internet protocol token that clearly could function as a currency. The computer science of Bitcoin derived from the structure and possibilities of networked machines. In the 1980s and 1990s, computer scientists outlined the possibilities of a public "distributed ledger" of replications of digital data. The Bitcoin white paper proposed that computers working on replicating items in a public distributed ledger or "chain" could encrypt one-way transactions. Each data development could be "hashed" or coded to a private account, which in turn could be stored by the owner or offered up on the distributed ledger in a transfer to another hashed account. Crucially, as such processing proceeds, the world of networked computers comes into in necessary agreement that each development in the chain has taken place. The possibilities of digital money were made manifest. In January 2009, the writer of the Bitcoin white paper released a "Bitcoin Code" that rewarded those who processed confirmations of Bitcoin transactions in more Bitcoin, a process that became known as "mining" (its practitioners are "miners"). The Bitcoin Code also limited, by the consent of the global network community, the total number of Bitcoin to 21 million. Transactions in Bitcoin began. The first of them appears to have been for a pizza.

Who created Bitcoin is one of the great mysteries of our age. The author of the white paper was Satoshi Nakamoto, a *nom de plume*. People close to the author (if not, possibly, the author) included top stars in the computer science firmament, such as Hal Finney of the California Institute of Technology. Nonetheless, among the early adopters and advocates of Bitcoin were a variety of down-and-outers. Young men squatting in their parents' basements—that archetype of the soft labor market of the slow-growth twenty-first century—were the face of Bitcoin accumulators and miners. The miners doing the mining that takes place with each Bitcoin transaction, per the protocol; computer users (many now automated) around the world verifying and completing each transaction for more Bitcoin by solving increasingly complex algorithms; here was the Bitcoin *demimonde*. Young people in basements in the aftermath of the Great Recession mining Bitcoin—this is what happens, what society deserves, when slow economic growth meets computer weirdness. Such was the general view with respect to Bitcoin on or about the early second decade of the 2000s.

Bitcoin initially sold for under a cent. To buy Bitcoin, one got onto the offbeat network and offered fiat currency—government-issued money like the United States dollar, via a bank account, for example—and bid an amount near the last price recorded in the online ledger to whoever might sell to you. If your bid was accepted, you got the Bitcoin in your "wallet." This was a computer account with a password. If you lost the password, you lost the Bitcoin (and so did the world). Exchanges began to materialize such that a third party could be a custodian for your Bitcoin. Coinbase, for example, opened in 2012.

Bitcoin swung wildly in price in its early days, if ultimately in an arc of serious appreciation. From thirty cents it went, in 2011, to three dollars, then thirty dollars, lurching down again, then back up to fifty dollars and even $1,000 in 2013. Then it went back down to $175. After the first nearly 90 percent crash from $1,000 in 2013, Bitcoin went reliably up, into the low thousands in early 2017. It spiked to $20,000 late that year and settled back in the single-digit thousands. In 2020, it broke out, powering past $65,000, only to go into another "crypto winter" (as the term goes) back to 2017 levels before breaking out past $65,000 again.

The notorious swinging price of the early days of Bitcoin gave rise to the pet internet meme of Bitcoin users. This is the word "HODL" in all caps. Late one night in December 2013, on the message board Bitcointalk, some Bitcoin trader with a profile picture of someone who looks like the actor James Van Der Beek made a post called "I AM HODLING." The young man—contextual clues from the profile picture and the text in the post indicate a young man—proceeded to spew out why he was holding. He realized that he had misspelled the word in the title of the post and that trying to correct it over and over while drunk did not work. The post began:

> I type d that tyitle twice because I knew it was
> wrong the first time. Still wrong. w/e. GF's out

at a lesbian bar, BTC crashing WHY AM I HOLDING? I'LL TELL YOU WHY.

And then he told us why. The basic reason was that:

I'M A BAD TRADER. Yeah you good traders can spot the highs and the lows pit pat piffy wing wong wang just like that and make a millino bucks sure no problem bro. Likewise the weak hands are like OH NO IT'S GOING DOWN I'M GONNA SELL.

And so on into the night. About this fellow, one can say that he had a girlfriend but that his pull with her was not sufficient to ward her off from contrary pursuits. He was at home, hit the bottle (he goes on about both "whisky" and "whiskey"), and did not count himself among the favored few who had a natural flair for trading and investments. This message board poster was no Wall Street type. He was an aspiring day (and night, as the Bitcoin market never closes) trader in Bitcoin. HODL soon became the darling word in Bitcoin culture on chat sites. That is what I am doing with Bitcoin; I am HODLING.[6]

In 2021, economic commentator Jeffrey A. Tucker reflected on his experience over the years with the Bitcoin community. He said that at Bitcoin conferences early on, in 2013–14, he saw Ferraris and Maseratis. People who had mined Bitcoin at eight cents or bought it at twenty dollars cashed out in 2013 at $1,000, perhaps, and bought a sports car. They spent their millino bucks. Eight years later, Tucker found the Ferrari and

---

[6] GameKyuubi, "I AM HODLING," Bitcointalk, Dec. 18, 2013, at nowbitcointalk.org/index.php?topic=375643.0. In internet patois, HODL can also mean "hold on for dear life."

Maseratis gone within the growing "crypto" subworld. This was even as Bitcoin had just powered past $40,000. People had realized, Tucker saw, that for the first time in the memory of "no one alive," they were dealing in "a deflationary currency," the contrary of "Gresham's law" in which bad money drives out good. The consequences were life-altering.

Tucker continued:

> If you are holding an inflationary asset [that depreciates in value, such as the United States dollar in the twentieth and twenty-first centuries], you have greater incentive to spend today rather than save, since you can reasonably expect the monetary unit to decline in value over time. You are also more likely to borrow and live beyond your means, because you service the loan in cheaper money than you receive (all else equal).

> How does this psychology change if you are holding a monetary asset that grows in value over time? Here you have an incentive not only to save but to seriously rethink the whole of your life habits. It influences whether you buy or rent, get a government job or take a risk in the markets, have children or not. All of this depends on one's assessment of one's future purchasing power, which is bound up with the anticipated value direction of a currency unit.

> This is sure enough what happened to the Bitcoin community three years after that nutty conference….
>
> This was when a new ethos suddenly hit the community. They became extremely frugal. They would look around at the junk in their houses and think what it could be worth in terms of Bitcoin. They rethought vacations. Shop in thrift stores. Move to a cheaper neighborhood. Buy a used car. Stop eating out….
>
> The Bitcoin rich began to live like the dollar poor.

"Time is money," as in the adage popularized by Benjamin Franklin. Because of fantastic increases in productive capabilities over the last several hundred years, modern people can be liberal with their time, binge-watching television and the like. We can spend less on productive activity—earning money—and more on consumption and leisure—spending money—because money is more valuable than in the past. It is more valuable because the time we do spend on productive activity yields far more product than a unit of time spent that way in the past, before the Industrial Revolution.[7]

If money loses value, it makes our increased time efficiency useless. If we get better at doing things and therefore can earn an equivalent amount in ten minutes as what used to take an hour, everything is ruined if money loses value. If the money earned in the ten minutes depreciates, why work the ten

---

[7] Jeffrey Tucker, "A Currency that Rises in Value Will Change Everything," American Institute for Economic Research, Feb. 12, 2021, at www.aier.org/article/a-currency-that-rises-in-value-will-change-everything/.

minutes so well? When Judas betrayed Jesus for thirty pieces of silver, thirty pieces of silver were, again, six months' wages. Six months' wages today, on average compensation, is far more than thirty pieces of silver (about $700 as of the early 2020s). A stable value of money is an encouragement to get better at using our time to make money. It has taken Bitcoin for this lesson, once so fundamental to the American experience—it certainly was to Benjamin Franklin—to be apparent to Americans in the contemporary period. For the historically minded, what happened to the Bitcoin community in the transformation Jeffrey Tucker described was a reclamation of the way life used to be in the United States.

Bitcoin should come as no surprise to any dedicated student of American history. How money was defined, who issued it, and how it came to be used throughout the economy were, for the better part of that history, amply open questions in American society. The point is obvious from any study of American economic and financial history from before the Civil War—if not from before the Great Depression of merely ninety years ago. Yet Bitcoin is a surprise to modern sensibilities. It appears to be offensive to elites and the managerial class. Especially in its early years after 2008, it seemed insufferably odd, down-and-out, suggestive of the weird fringes of computer science, and something that crept out of the idleness and exasperation of the Great Recession. Since the 1960s, primary and secondary education has done away with the standard American history textbook lessons emphasizing monetary history—something every average participant in the democracy debated and discussed routinely in eras previous to our own. Interminable chapters on silver ratios and grains of gold were once staple fare in the textbooks. Perhaps if we were educated in the old way, Bitcoin would not be such a shock. It is the purpose of this book to show that Bitcoin is perfectly compatible, uncannily compatible, with the rhythms of American monetary history across the whole of that history.

Bitcoin's resonance with American monetary history is indeed so strong that it is reasonable to perceive in Bitcoin the force of history. Bitcoin corresponds positively to the first half of American monetary history and negatively to the second half. In the first half, roughly 1789–1913, the federal government largely stayed out of the business of manufacturing money outside of making coins, and let competitive private entities have at it in making the nation's currency. Feedback loops linked together these private entities, keeping the supply of money consistent with the demand and prices stable as economic growth boomed. When people opted to use one bank's currency over that of another, redeemed currency for precious metal or vice versa, or applied for bank loans or refrained from doing so, it was a signal to all involved about how much money to produce and for whom. Today, the essential connecting tissue of these feedback loops has been lost. Nobody uses one issuer's United States dollar over another's, because private currency is now subject to taxation and regulation from which the Federal Reserve Note is exempt. Nobody redeems currency for precious metal or some other definitional asset, because currency now lacks formal definition, and gold and silver (and Bitcoin) transitions are subject to taxation. So people use the government money. This in turn gives the government more purchasing power and shrinks the size and operating room of the private, the real economy.

In the second half of American monetary history, basically from 1913 to the present, the government took over the monetary system. It shouldered aside all private currency issuers (who had previously been dominant), downgraded the role of private clearinghouses and lenders of last resort, put taxes on non-government money, and set up institutions (above all, the Federal Reserve) indicating its view that running the money system should be a matter of largely governmental professionals and bureaucracy. Bitcoin holds—HODLS—within it an implicit critique of these two halves of American monetary history. It vindicates the idea that currency should be privately made in a competitive free market. And by virtue of both its architecture and culture—piffy wing wong wang—Bitcoin also dismisses the modern contention that professionals, PhDs at the Federal Reserve, for example, who lack direct accountability for their actions, should control the monetary system. No feedback loop hits the PhDs with force when the Fed makes a decision. Bitcoin, that novelty of the twenty-first century, functions as an affirmation of the first half of American monetary history and a criticism of the second half.

Bitcoin therefore has attributes suggesting that it is functioning as both the memory of American monetary history and the agent of a leading edge of the force of that history and heritage in the present. It is as if the nation understands, somewhere in its consciousness, that it has resources within its own experience to reestablish the original and longstanding monetary foundations of the economy if it wishes to. Bitcoin indicates a nostalgia for the way things used to be, monetarily. Psychologists speak of the experience of "rumination," in which a person thinks over and over again about some past mistake or missed opportunity. The counsel is to overcome rumination by seeing how the hurt of a past transition provides an opportunity for improvement in the present and future. In the uncanny way that Bitcoin appears to both endorse the first half of American monetary history and throw up a formidable critique of the second half, it is as if the collective consciousness of the nation is ruminating on its own experiential resources to forge a positive way forward in the twenty-first century. Walt Whitman spoke of the "barbaric yawp" as the quintessential cry of the optimistic American. Bitcoin is more than that—it is computer science. Bitcoin is the pinnacle—for now—of the information technology revolution's representation of the principles of classical sound money. But it is a barbaric yawp as well. This is quite a combination. It is as if history has coalesced into a moment, as latent forces of the ideal of the American Dream strive to reassert their privileges and reclaim their primacy.

America's forgotten monetary history

Prior to 1913 and the founding of the Federal Reserve System, American currency—the dollar—held its value against the goods and services that it could very reliably be used to acquire. By modern reconstructions, the consumer price index, or the average price of everything in the economy, was flat for the century or so prior to 1913. The only serious change came during and after the Civil War. The price level doubled and then sank to par from 1861 to 1879. This was a logical outcome of the demand boom (from war production) and the supply constraint (of young men leaving the labor force to go off to war). Otherwise, a loaf of bread, a pair of overalls, rent for rooms—the price of such everyday things stayed the same nominal amount, in dollars, decade after decade before 1913. Consistency of this nature gave rise to an expression now never heard: "sound as a dollar."

In such a day—again, the normal circumstance in the United States for the better part of the 125 years before 1913—setting a goal of making and saving money had real significance. Money that a person made had value and would retain value. The consequences for the economy were profound. On modern reconstructions, economic growth was regularly 4 or 5 percent per year in the century and a quarter to 1913. This is more than double the American growth rate of the 2000s. Prior to 1913, Americans threw themselves into productive work and saving. The American economy, consequently, became both the largest in the world and, by any reasonable metric, the greatest in the history of the world. Population growth was astounding. In 1790, the population of Chicago was nil. In 1900, it was 1.7 million.

The roll of economic achievements from this era is impressive in the extreme. For example, in the industrious years prior to 1913, the American economy (building on the precedents of the global Agricultural Revolution) solved the ancient food supply problem. Tremendous advances in farming techniques, from the mechanical reaper to the tractor engine, made labor less and less necessary on plots of arable land. Transportation innovations enabled the best land to be devoted to farming, the food to then be shipped to market, and the rest of the land to be devoted to new purposes, exponentially increasing economic potential. A tinkerer on one of the farm engines, Henry Ford, realized the implications for personal transportation and invented the mass global car industry. The building construction that took place in the United States at this time was another prodigious achievement. Older towns in the United States, typically those in states with an income tax (which keeps those places bereft of new investment), still show off the waves of housing and factory structures built in the nineteenth and early twentieth centuries. These were the first homes networked for everything save the smart grid today. Knitting together community after community with electric power, water and sewage, gas, and telephone systems was another achievement of this era. The economic accomplishments in this vein go on and on. They are the stuff of the great American economic renaissance of the period before 1913.

Since 1913, American money has not been "good and sound." The average price of consumer goods has increased absurdly since that time, by at least thirtyfold. The increases came in waves. Sometimes prices increased fantastically. At their lowest, the increases were not the old standard level of nil, but sure and steady. Inflation totaled 100 percent from 1913 to 1920, 70 percent from 1940 to 1950, and 200 percent from 1966 to 1982. Otherwise, prices have increased by 1–3 percent per year. (The only deflation to speak of was in the early 1930s.) Even a 1 percent inflation means that over a generation, thirty years, the value of saved money goes down by 35 percent. One dollar saved in 1913 bought fifty cents worth of stuff in 1920. One dollar saved in 1940 bought sixty cents worth of stuff in 1950. A dollar saved in 1966 bought thirty-three cents of stuff in 1982. Over these thirty-three combined years, one dollar turned into ten cents.

An essential fact about the old-time American economy remains widely unknown and unappreciated today. Paper currency was largely privately issued. A five-dollar bill in 1840—privately issued. A fifty in 1905, or a ten-spot in 1888—government paper dollar notes competed with private paper dollar notes at these points in time (and in general from 1862 to 1913). The federal government of the United States did not churn out currency as the dollar's sole issuer until the late date of 1935, when private paper dollar issuance ceased. And care of a simultaneous executive order of President Franklin D. Roosevelt—a patrician who had worked but shortly in the private sector—the federal government confiscated all private holdings of gold and eliminated the freedom to hold gold thereafter.

The government's not acting as a monopoly currency issuer was consistent with the Constitution of 1789, which is silent on the matter. The legal concept *expressio unius est exclusio alterius*—when one thing in a class is mentioned, others in that class are excluded—is interesting in this context. What the United States did was define the dollar, as an ounce of precious metal such as silver or one-twentieth of an ounce of gold. The idea that the government would print or otherwise create currency, let alone monopolize the printing and issuance of currency (even well-meaning monopolies lack good feedback loops), is not a constitutional one in any conventional sense. For fully more than the first half of the history of the United States, innumerable (typically over a thousand) private entities, as profit-making businesses, produced currency and offered it to the public directly. Under the auspices of this kind of natural and constitutional monetary system for over a century, the United States climbed up to its status as the greatest economy in the history of the world. Clearly, having a private money system beholden to the people, as opposed to politicians or bureaucrats on a daily basis, was not a fatal flaw for the economy of the United States. It grew to be the greatest the world had ever seen when private money reigned supreme.

The Constitution does not speak of currency. Rather, it gives "power" to Congress to "coin Money" and "regulate the Value thereof." English kings occasionally had tyrannical power to monopolize money; the United States government did not. From the outset, Congress interpreted this money clause plainly. With the Coinage Act of 1792, it set up an agency, the United States Mint, to strike metal into coins with values imprinted on them. Here, Congress exercised both parts of the power in the clause. Congress struck metal into coin (the first part) and said what each coin was worth (the "regulate the Value thereof" part). With this act, Congress gave Americans a place where they could—if they wished—bring precious metals, namely gold and silver, to turn them into money. The Mint would take the metal, strike it into coins with values specified on the face, and then return the coins to the person who brought the metal. If you offered an ounce of silver, the Mint would take a little off, replace it with a base metal, strike the amalgam into a coin that read "one dollar," and give it to you with the residual silver. If you offered a half ounce of gold, the Mint would do the same and strike it into a coin that read "ten dollars" and give it to you with the residual gold.

In its heady original days of economic growth and agricultural and industrial revolution, the United States coined money—but it did not produce currency. Currency was an affair of the marketplace. Currency was a piece of paper saying that the issuer would redeem, on demand, that piece of paper for coin in the amount of the denomination of the currency. A twenty-dollar bill meant that the bearer could go to the issuer and get twenty dollars in coin—produced by the Mint or whoever else.

Two characteristics of this arrangement are perhaps strange to the modern observer. They both have to do with the concept of *offering*. The first characteristic is that everything here was voluntary. Everything was consensual. The Mint *offered* itself as a coiner of money, one of a number in the country. The other mints were private. The United States Mint was a business like any other, presenting its services for a fee. The fee the Mint charged for its service was the little bit of precious metal it kept, replacing that bit with a base metal when coining the gold or silver. If people wanted to bring their precious metals to the Mint for coining, they were free to. They were just as free to do something else with their precious metal. This included taking that metal for striking to a private mint, setting up a mint themselves, or using the metal for something else. The Mint had to keep in mind its competitive position. Its fee had to be a market rate. And its service had to be as good as that of the competition and alternative uses for metal.

The second characteristic was the nature of the "dollar." The United States *offered* the dollar as a definition, no more and no less. Congress proposed a twentieth of an ounce of gold or, alternatively, an ounce of silver as the definition of a dollar. If someone else wanted to offer a definition of a dollar or offer some other name for a basic monetary unit, they were free to. Congress felt that it was a public service, one not exclusive to the government, to suggest a basic monetary unit to the public. If the people wished to use it, they could. If they did not wish to use it, including if they wished to make a definition of a dollar on their own, that was their prerogative. The dollar, for its part, was essentially equivalent to the prevailing monetary unit at the time. This was the eight-piece Spanish real, also an ounce of silver.

Aside from offering definitions of base monetary units and a place where one could get money coined, the monetary system was the affair of the private sector. Paper money, currency, coins not struck by the Mint, all this was left to well up naturally within the marketplace. Under the auspices of this largely private and organic system, for a century and a quarter, the American economy grew and prospered like no other ever had.

After Congress authorized the Federal Reserve in 1913, the United States started printing its own currency on a permanent basis. This was the "Federal Reserve Note," first series 1914, that dominates global currency issuance today. By 1935, the United States had all but outlawed currency other than the Federal Reserve Note. The United States has done well enough since 1913. It remained the richest country in the world and the homeland of the American Dream. But it had negative experiences unlike anything seen before. The Great Depression of the 1930s had no peer in the nineteenth century. The 1970s stagflation, in which the price level tripled and stayed high for good, had no like. And sub-2 percent economic growth sustained for decades, a feature of the 2000s, was unknown in the era prior to 1913.

Bitcoin, cryptocurrency, and distributed ledger or blockchain technology are offering—*offering* again—an alternative vision of the future of money and currency. They are offering, perhaps inchoately, an opportunity for the forces of natural economic creativity to reclaim the prerogatives of making money and currency. Making money here is meant in the simple sense—manufacturing or otherwise creating money for use. This was always an affair of the private sector. That it has not been for now more than a century since 1913 has been exceptional.

In *Free Money*, we offer a monetary history of the United States in view of the challenge that is arising today from Bitcoin and cryptocurrency. Our sense is that Bitcoin in particular represents an attempt to reclaim the original currency tradition of the United States—the currency tradition whose associated economic development lifted that country, as well as a great part of the world, into mass prosperity. Bitcoin has properties uncannily like gold. It is fixed in ultimate supply and difficult to get anew, it can be used for transactions but only with some difficulty, and it has primordial and cult-like appeal. It all but presents itself as a new gold—a new store of value, a new store of time. Meanwhile, other cryptos, perhaps beginning with Ether and various "stablecoins," offer themselves as inspirations from Bitcoin that might prove practical in facilitating the exchange of goods and services. Here is "coined" money, and from it, currencies.

What we may well be experiencing is a mass social-psychological attempt, on the part of the global movement propelling cryptos forward, to revert the dominant monetary system of the world to the beneficial conditions of its *status quo ante*. In the terms of social psychologist Carl Jung, the collective unconscious across humanity, in the 2020s, is requiring that good arrangements that it knows are in the past, in the positive experience of the species, be brought to the fore for beneficial purposes again. From this perspective, it is appropriate to note that no matter its origins in computer science, Bitcoin as a movement rose up from below, frankly from people who might be hectored as losers and nerds. The professional class is satisfied with modern monetary arrangements. But the people, the masses as they used to be called, are not satisfied, for whatever ultimately unanalyzable and aboriginal reason. And through their homely as opposed to professional processes, they are striving to force change.

Such observations are, of course, speculative. What can be done on an empirical basis is history. It is rather clear that the pre-1913 monetary history of the United States comports well with the contours of foundational monetary reform as outlined by the Bitcoin and cryptocurrency phenomena. It used to be that the definition of money was up for grabs. The public availed itself of definitions that it felt worked best. It used to be that the question of who issued money was the same question as who produced anything in the economy—namely, anyone who is good at it. And it used to be that there was explicit profit in making money and currency.

This was so not only in the United States, but globally. In currency arrangements before the World War of 1914, private banks issued, in the main, even king currencies such as the British pound sterling. The resonance that Bitcoin has with the extended early part of American monetary history is a resonance it has with the monetary history of many places, to be sure. A focus on America is, however, probably necessary. The United States dollar became the indisputable global currency in the mid-twentieth century. This never changed well into the twenty-first century. It was a remarkable development, in that federal authorities ended all possibility of dollar redemption in gold decades ago, in 1971. Such an action would have killed off any other currency. Somehow, the dollar, from the 1970s to the 2020s, defied the common fate of fiat currencies (of being shunned) and found global supremacy as a floating currency for fifty years. This is a unique event in global monetary history—and, as such, probably primed not to last. The notion that alternatives to fiat currencies, ones abiding by classical definitions of money, will not strike back against the post-1971 order is untenable. Bitcoin came for the dollar, came for it in a competitive and challenging sense.

To Bitcoin's connection to American monetary history we now turn. If we knew our American history well, perhaps Bitcoin would not seem an odd and scruffy development. Perhaps it would be seen as a perfectly understandable, natural, and necessary development. It is as if we are half-educated about and half-aware of American monetary history. We grasp the latter half of this history and think it is normative. The standard view is that monetary issuance is a normal monopoly of the government. Governments issue currency. If someone else does, it is foolish, crank-like, and possibly criminal. Another standard view, if a little strained in contemporary times, is that a government "backs" its currency. It did so, we think, not very long ago (prior to 1971) in gold, the most classical store of value. Now it does so, we think, by such things as its own creditworthiness. These views pertain to the muddied monetary consciousness of the world after 1913 and 1935 and 1971. They do not pertain to the world before those times. And that earlier era is that in which the United States grew to be the largest economy in the world, a rise that occurred at the peak of the global Industrial Revolution.

The service we wish to provide in this book is a recovery of the traditional monetary history of the United States in view of the rising challenge of Bitcoin. A conclusion to draw from this history is that American monetary history is, overall, in accord with Bitcoin. This is a matter of some importance. If Bitcoin is, in central respects, consistent with American monetary history, then its prospects are perhaps greater than we are apt to imagine. History provides no bar to developments as Bitcoin is outlining. Indeed, Bitcoin is building upon history, trying to compel current affairs to move back along the natural direction staked out by history. By clarifying how this is the case—by investigating American monetary history with respect to Bitcoin—we can be in a better position to continue to deal with Bitcoin, perhaps even to welcome, improve, and spur on this fascinating phenomenon of our age.

CHAPTER 2

The Industrial Revolution—In Money

First, the Agricultural and then the Industrial Revolutions—what enormous developments in human history. In Western societies, about four hundred years ago, food production and transportation techniques improved such that agriculture could sustain large numbers of people in non-farm occupations. This made possible the Industrial Revolution. The Agricultural Revolution emerged, in ways that remain mysterious, in the seventeenth century, probably in the vast Noble Republic of Poland and Lithuania, the biggest country in Europe at the time. Traders on the Baltic Sea began to bring surfeits of foodstuffs from the Noble Republic westward, clueing in English farmers in particular that they could learn more efficient ways of going about their work. English farm yields soon sharply increased, which opened up opportunities for a whole new world of non-agricultural production. Over the centuries into modern times, farming went from occupying nearly all workers to 1 percent of workers.

The great "take-off," as it was called by British economic historian Phyllis Deane, of the Industrial Revolution dates from about 1750. Thereafter, for decade upon decade, all sorts of new products and devices appeared in economic life, first in England and ultimately everywhere. The quintessential example was the steam engine—of which there were so many variations, each one improving on the other in some way, that we cannot specify an ur-product or an inventor. Other new products of life-changing significance included all sorts of "shuttles" that loomed raw wool, cotton, and silk into fabric in a fraction of the time that would have otherwise been needed. Clever mining equipment and techniques brought forth metals that could be fashioned into new goods, as well as fuel that could heat furnaces so that these metals could be shaped and engines run. Advances in consumer goods brought an abundance of niceties, such as decorative tableware, into vast numbers of homes as population growth boomed.

The Industrial Revolution's supreme chronicler, the historian David S. Landes (1924–2013), summarized the great event this way. With the Industrial Revolution, on a large scale, "there was a substitution of mechanical devices for human skills," and "inanimate power…took the place of human and animal strength." Machines fashioned things, and machines powered things, freeing up human labor for other pursuits. Furthermore, it was not a blip. There was no reversion to the trend, but the establishment of a new trend. Beginning with the great take-off, a cumulative process was engaged whereby the living standards of each previous age came to be exceeded as a matter of course.[8]

---

[8] David S. Landes, *The Unbound Prometheus: Technological Change and Industrial Development in Western Europe from 1750 to the Present* (Cambridge: Cambridge University Press, 1969), 1.

The Industrial Revolution spread past England. The new United States saw its economic growth surge for good in the years after the founding of its constitutional government in 1789. This was so even as the United States maintained political hostility against the United Kingdom. Once France, in 1815, took leave of its focus on political revolution and Napoleonic conquest, it settled into an imitation of British economic success. The term "industrial revolution" was coined, in French, in the 1820s. From the 1850s on, Japan and Germany got intensely involved in the cumulative process of industrial and material development. By modern accounting, all these places were growing at permanent rates of 4 or 5 percent per year, meaning that their economies produced twice as much every half generation. Such metrics, however, do not capture the half of it—in that so much of the growth came in new, previously undreamt-of products and services that people discovered were useful and pleasing. The kerosene lamp, the Mason jar, off-the-rack clothes, one new thing after another kept on coming in the era of the Industrial Revolution.

The number and variety of products increased enormously with the Industrial Revolution. Demographics experienced a similar transformation. In 1650, the world population was probably about 500 million persons, twice what there had been in 1000. In 1776, China had about 250 million inhabitants, and the United States 2.5 million. By 1800, there were nearly a billion persons globally, and by 1900, nearly 1.75 billion. In the places central to the Industrial Revolution, the growing population saw comprehensive changes in the ways of living and working. People moved from farms to cities and worked in factories and in buildings, making things and providing services. Previously, work was chiefly outdoors or in barns and at hearths, producing and storing food and husbanding farmland and farm animals. The amount of new things—of "stuff"—was phenomenally greater by 1900 compared to 1650. There were many more persons on the earth, they mainly concentrated and specialized on making things that were not food—even though food production increased fantastically—and they lived in ever greater proportion in cities and towns as opposed to on agricultural plots and in villages.

The transition was wrenching and unpleasant in myriad ways, to be sure. The uprooting of centuries of tradition based on mass life on the land, in the era of the Industrial Revolution, was momentous and unwelcome and disorienting in many cases. Religion experienced a huge popular upsurge as the epochal transitions of the Industrial Revolution proceeded. Churches and religious schools were built like crazy as industrial workers and their families retrofitted daily religious practices of the farm and hearth for urban circumstances. Just as certainly, life became easier and richer with the Industrial Revolution. Average wages steadily increased, the amount of work needed for subsistence went consistently down (a key element of flourishing societies), and the growing population had larger and larger stashes of "stuff" (and lifestyle options) beyond what had been available before.

The bottom line—an idiom derived from accounting, a profession that also took off with the Industrial Revolution—is that the amount of stuff increased absurdly from circa 1750 to 1900. All that stuff could be, and was, exchanged for money. This means that the market for money, as the Industrial Revolution got going and sustained itself, felt a pressure and an opportunity like never before.

Calculus and alchemy

A most intriguing question about the Industrial Revolution is where its money came from. Certainly, there was not an increase in the standard and received forms of money, in gold and silver coin, similar to the enormous increase in economic growth. There were diversions of gold from the New World to the Old, but no total increase on the scale of economic growth during the Industrial Revolution. That would have been a physical impossibility.

Whatever the genius of the Industrial Revolution in mining and metallurgy, it could not increase the stock of precious metals available to it by 4 or 5 percent per year on a permanent basis. There could not be twice as much total precious metals every half generation. Yet precious metals had been the basis of monetary exchange for centuries and millennia. New techniques of gold mining and production were achieved during the Industrial Revolution, certainly, but they were minuscule in comparison to its other achievements. As the inimitable scholar of the gold standard Nathan Lewis has found, over the extended nineteenth century, from 1775 to 1900, the increase in the world's stock of gold increased maybe by 3.5- or 4.5-fold. In the United States, the increase in money, bank notes, and all dollar media together was 163-fold—as the gold price in dollars stayed stable. "The money supply increased by 163 times," Lewis exclaimed, "while the value of money was stable" in gold, which was barely increasing at all in total stock, comparatively. The huge increase in the money supply, as each unit of the money supply retained value in gold, reflected that the products and services exchangeable for money had become phenomenally more abundant.[9]

Shortly before the Industrial Revolution approached its take-off, in the late seventeenth century, Isaac Newton, along with Gottfried Leibniz, clarified mathematical wisdom that had been outlined in the Middle Ages, including in India, about the nature of rates of growth. Newton elaborated the "infinitesimal calculus" that showed how curves that increasingly slope up—curves representing rates of growth—may be understood as being held up by the space beneath them. How much a curve was increasing or decreasing, its slope at any moment, was its "differentiation." How much space below it was its "integration." These became the two central concepts of the discipline of calculus. How apt they were to the Industrial Revolution that was about to emerge in England and then the world. There were about to be high rates of change in economic growth—the differential—and these rates would accumulate such that the process was sustained—the integral.

Intriguingly, as he spelled out his calculus, Newton undertook an intensive investigation, relevant to his capacity as England's Master of the Mint, into the science of producing gold from other elements. He determined that alchemy was impossible.

Newton's twin projects, in calculus and in alchemy, captured the relationship that was about to obtain between the Industrial Revolution and the time-honored form of money.

---

9   Nathan Lewis, "The 'Money Supply' with a Gold Standard," New World Economics, Jan. 2, 2010, at www.newworldeconomics.com/the-money-supply-with-a-gold-standard. Cf. statistics this author cited in Lewis, *Gold: The Final Standard* (New Berlin, NY: Canyon Maple Publishing, 2017), 255n64, namely James Turk, "The Aboveground Gold Stock: Its Importance and Size," Gold Money Foundation, 2012, 14.

The Industrial Revolution would provide an illustration of the calculus, as it established a rate of increase for the economy at an exponential rate. The increase in the quantity of gold, and each example of a precious metal, would in turn plod along like a turtle. The increase in the stock of gold would only budge even with the innovations of the Industrial Revolution. This illustrated and proved Newton's conjecture. Alchemy was beyond all hope. The integrals of the two rates of growth represented their respective mass accumulations. There would be an enormous amount of new material goods in the economy and an amount of gold not much more than before. A new ratio would emerge: ever-increasing creation of material things over a little extra gold.

Just before the outset of the Industrial Revolution, it had been fully worked out—by Isaac Newton no less, and in his capacity as a high financial official—that an increase in the stock of money in the form of gold could never match that of a system of exponential growth. In short order, such a system arrived in the realm of economic output. The Industrial Revolution took off, and gold production, as Newton knew it would, only inched along. The Industrial Revolution occurred under an understanding—the Newtonian understanding—that the stock of gold would never keep pace. The twin pursuits that Newton had in math and alchemy were a perfect schematic anticipation of what unfolded in the economy, and in its basic financing and transaction instrument, in the generations after his death in 1727.

Newton's juxtaposition was perhaps the central monetary fact of the Industrial Revolution. Indeed, it is one of the keys that opened up the possibilities of the Industrial Revolution. Today, there is a common misapprehension that gold-based monetary systems constrain economic growth. Egged on by modern monetary experts, people can think that in a gold-based monetary system, gold must increase at the same rate of economic growth. We will be incapable of understanding the Industrial Revolution—indeed, economic growth in general, including in our own day—if we harbor this belief. As Newton showed as the Industrial Revolution was about to begin its march, it was to be clearly understood that the supply of gold could never keep up with the supply of an economy in a highly productive mode.

This did not mean that gold (along with other precious metals) would have to lose its monetary role—far from it. Rather, it meant that the great part of the new quantity, the new supply, of money needed to finance and enable the trans-actions of the Industrial Revolution would have to come from some source other than gold and precious metals. What would become paramount was not the quantity of gold and precious metals, but their price (and even, more conceptually, the value of time they represented). Quantity would come from some new monetary innovation. The price of gold would come to represent how much people wanted it as opposed to the new media of exchange—currencies, or what was "current" in mar-ketplaces for regular transactions.

If the price of gold was low, it meant that people were per-fectly content to use the new currencies, and that these were functioning well as finance and purchasing devices for all the new stuff. If the price of gold was high, it meant that people were not so content to use the new currencies. Inevitably, in these cases, because of the limited quantity of gold, this meant that there was an economic depression. And if the price of gold was stable—invariably at a low price—it meant that the new currencies were consistently proving useful as transaction devices in an ever-booming Industrial Revolution economy.

The spontaneous innovation

In eras previous to the Industrial Revolution, economic growth was generally no greater than the ability of the economy to generate more precious metals. An economy growing at half a percent per year had a fair chance of mining half a percent more precious metals than already existed. Indeed, any economic growth that did occur reliably called forth the demand for more precious metals, in that existing money, in the absence of new money, became more valuable with every episode of economic growth. There was a close relationship between economic growth and the ability to acquire new precious metals. The more the former increased, the more the latter was pushed until that rate was matched, the magnitudes on modern standards being small.

It is not entirely correct to say that monetary metals had a price. It is more accurate to say that they provided the means for the definition of money. They were a standard that all mutually recognized. Money, in ancient and medieval times, was commonly thought of in terms of weights of precious metals. A fraction of a pound (Latin: libra) of silver counted as one English monetary unit, the pound sterling. Twenty silver shillings (or minted pieces of silver adding up to a quarter of a pound in weight) was deemed, because of common usage, the monetary equivalent of one-quarter of an ounce of minted gold. Both quantities defined the monetary unit of the pound sterling, or £. In the early years of the United States, federal authorities defined just under an ounce of gold at twenty dollars and just under an ounce of silver at one dollar. Therefore, the United Kingdom–United States currency exchange rate was approximately four-to-one. These determinations emerged historically from the use of various weights of precious metals over the ages as units of exchange.

The definitions were largely unchanging. Setting aside comparatively minor variations that arose from time to time, an ounce of gold minted in London was eighty shillings, which together made up a pound of silver. In the United States, minted silver coins had fifteen times the precious metal per denomination of minted gold coins.

An amount of money expressed as a weight of a precious metal was a rule—rule in the homely sense, as in the word "ruler" describing a stick with inches marked off on it. Money as a weight of metal was an identity, like two sides of an equation are an identity. Twelve inches made a foot, 231 cubic inches a (United States) gallon, and vice versa. Just under an ounce of silver was a dollar, twenty of those pieces was an ounce of gold, and vice versa. How weights and measures were defined and how money was defined did not differ. There was nothing to contend with or debate about. Monetary denominations of precious metals were specifications of weight. The denominations given on a coin certified how much a certain metal inhered in that given stamped disc made largely of that metal.

It would not have followed, in a world of money as material weights, to expect that if there were a sharp and lasting increase in the availability of all other goods (especially in immaterial "goods" like services, which on account of their immateriality can be provided in ever greater number and quality), the sum of the weights of available precious metals—their very masses— would increase proportionately.

Prior to the Industrial Revolution, this interesting matter did not require much thinking about. This is because economic growth rates in excess of the ability to mine more precious metals were rarely sustained. When, occasionally, the increase in the extractability of precious metals was greater than the rate of economic growth, mines went dormant until economic growth picked up. There was an easy relationship between precious metals, money, and the economy. The total stock in each category was capable of regularly changing in unison. In ancient and medieval times, as scientists and historians are increasingly discovering through ice-core analysis, the mining of new precious metals closely followed the patterns of economic growth.

All that ended with the Industrial Revolution. In this new era, expansion of products and services greatly exceeded the new quantities of precious metals. As all sorts of unimagined wares came to market while the Industrial Revolution took hold, not at all displacing existing useful items but adding to them, the ratio of material goods and productive services against precious metals shot way up for the duration.

In the face of this development, anticipated as it was by Newton, a spontaneous innovation—that great characteristic of the Industrial Revolution—took place. People decided to make money now that it was scarce. Economics should be comfortable with this thought. Economics is the study of the allocation of scarce resources. It is the job of commerce to innovate new methods of allocating scarce resources. People in the era of the Industrial Revolution made money in the homely sense, as captured by the Latin phrase *homo faber*. They fabricated it themselves. They coined money—requiring scarce metals—less and less in proportion to printing money—which required the un-scarce raw materials of paper and ink.

There was a link between the coined and the printed money. At any time, the bearer of printed money could take it back to whoever issued it, in exchange for the unit in which it was defined. For example, a ten-dollar piece of paper currency might specify that it was redeemable in silver. At any moment, the holder of that currency could return it to the currency's issuer. By the terms written on the currency, the holder would get just under ten ounces of silver for it. To the degree that such transactions were close to automatic—a holder brought in the currency and, sure enough, got the ten silver pieces right away—paper currency defined as claims on precious metals met the need for new money in the Industrial Revolution.

Paper devices roughly of this sort had existed for some time across the globe, in Qing China and Renaissance Italy, for example. Dutch traders of the seventeenth century regularly were able to use their letters of credit as currency. A merchant traveling to a faraway port to pick up wares for sale at home would carry a paper credit certificate that the recipient could readily offer to someone else as payment or collateral on a loan. Prior to the Industrial Revolution, such things were specialties of commercial enterprise. With the Industrial Revolution, they became a comprehensive necessity.

Conceivably, perhaps, the participants in the Industrial Revolution could have dealt with the divergence in growth rates that the great event brought in another way. The divergence was between the rate of increase in proliferating useful goods and services and that of recalcitrant precious metals. Participants in the economy could have acquiesced to a comprehensive, long-term deflation. If economic growth was to be 5 percent per year, and the most precious metal production could be bumped up to was perhaps 1 percent, there presumably would be a chronic 4 percent deflation. Things in general would be priced 4 percent less every year. People who held capital would hoard it. This is detrimental to an economy. Those who hold capital must deploy it for an economy not to decline (this is in good part what happened in the Great Depression of the 1930s).

If there were a 4 percent deflation year upon year, the monetary medium itself would gain in value in the absence of any improvement in its quality. Yet production of gold, silver, and all the rest was not particularly enhanced during the Industrial Revolution. Everything else was—the steam engines, spinning shuttles, and closets full of chinaware that came *ex nihilo* were the things that were enhanced during the Industrial Revolution. The volume of available food and the ability to transport product were the things that were enhanced. Gold remained gold, and silver remained silver, the same old things in quality and marginally increasing in quantity. It would have made little sense for something unimproved, in the context of mass improvement, to increase in value at a very healthy rate.

There was one other reason precious metals could not continue as the near-exclusive money supply in the Industrial Revolution. If the stock of precious metals could not increase at the rate of economic growth and was to remain the sole transaction instrument, this meant there would not be enough money where it needed to be. The distribution of precious metals would not correspond to the need for money in the newly burgeoning world of economic opportunity. Never in any economy is there enough precious metal in all locations in precise moments to settle all accounts when trades of goods and services occur. An example is transoceanic shipping. Gold crisscrossing the ocean all the time with the equivalent amount of wares going the other way is an absurdity.

Previously, the increasing precious metal supply could match, in total, the standard slower rates of economic growth. That extra supply entered into the global precious metals market and found where it would fetch the highest price. This was an essential part of the efficiency of the precious metal money system. The situation was different, however, when economic growth became permanently higher than the growth of the supply of precious metals. If precious metals were the only things used as money in this condition, there would be no natural process for money to get where it was most useful.

Current holders of money might be interested in directing their holdings to where they might make the largest return. Yet there was no guarantee of this—new production typically addresses the matter of a deficiency of supply against demand. What was certain was that there could not be a sufficiency of new producers, commensurate with the economic growth, whose purpose in producing new supplies of precious metals was to sell for the best price. When economic growth was small, the degree of entrepreneurialism in the production of new precious metals had corresponded to the degree of entrepreneurialism in the economy as a whole. Therefore, when Newton disproved alchemy, he also effectively proved that entrepreneurial genius in precious metal production could never match that of an economy that really got going.

There would have been an efficiency loss if the economy of the Industrial Revolution had acquiesced to a deflation corresponding to the supply of precious metals. This would have had no like in history, in that before, when precious metal production could keep up with economic growth, the outlets for new money were always there when a little growth beckoned. The populace of the Industrial Revolution understood, implicitly, that their historic take-off required a take-off in money production as well.

There is a need to belabor these points somewhat, because today, there is a general impression that money systems based on precious metals are a hostage to their supply. This reflects our lack of familiarity, including on the part of trained economists, with these systems. Precious metal money systems across the centuries have been price-stable and quantity-elastic. During the Industrial Revolution, the transition beyond a precious metal money stock happened organically, imperceptibly, and with little need for a theory of the system to be spelled out beforehand—whatever Newton's labors at the Mint.

Occasionally, there was theory spelled out beforehand. In 1729, for example, Benjamin Franklin published "The Nature and Necessity of a Paper-Currency." This essay observed that there was not enough gold and silver coin to support the natural commercial interest, in Philadelphia at the time, in such things as "Ship-Building" and "Labouring and Handicrafts." Franklin explained that Pennsylvania should allow paper money, in his recommendation redeemable in land. The industriousness Franklin saw all about him required it. Pennsylvania needed redeemable paper money to avoid such things as "Workmen" having to be "paid in Goods, because it is a great Disadvantage to them." In barter, one is paid in the particular good that the trading partner has. Money wages mean one is paid in the one good, in money, that is tradable for any other good.[10]

Building on the commercial system of certificates of credit, various institutions increasingly offered currency, or "notes,"

---

[10] Benjamin Franklin, "The Nature and Necessity of a Paper-Currency," April 3, 1729, National Archives Founders Online, at founders.archives.gov/documents/Franklin/01-01-02-0041.

that were redeemable back at the institution for their given amount, typically in precious metals. As the system developed by the late eighteenth century, if an institution issued a twenty-dollar note, the holder of that note got an ounce of gold on demand from that institution. These institutions—banks, though they could just as easily be merchant houses or private mints—sprouted up as the Industrial Revolution got going. Their proprietors saw the quickening of economic opportunity that was all about them and offered capital loans, in the form of these redeemable notes, to entrepreneurs who appeared to have good ideas in the propitious environment. The entrepreneurs took the notes and spent them on building up their businesses. The recipients of the notes either redeemed them or exchanged them for goods and services with another who was willing to accept the note.

This was the content of "monetary policy" before the rise of central banks. It was distinctly multi-nodal and unofficial. The arrangements had multiple feedback loops that communicated distinctly relevant information to different parties. The home bank knew if it was issuing too much or too little in notes on the basis of redemption requests; the recipients of the notes, exchanging goods or services, testified to how "current," or how generally accepted, this monetary medium (or "currency") was in real life; people who kept the notes (or shed them) testified to their belief of how much they were functioning as a store of value and as reliably redeemable in precious metal money. The system was efficient, flexible, and resilient, in important respects, on monetary policy criteria, superior to that of the latter-day central banks and bureaucratic monetary policy management.

There were innumerable money issuers "on the spot," in the language of free-market economist F. A. Hayek. The familiarity of local money issuers with the circumstances close to them made them realize who in the local entrepreneurial landscape they should consider for new note-issue loans. The useful clarity such a system provided was, as the price-stable economic growth of the nineteenth century would make clear, phenomenal. Good ideas attracted start-up money. With note-issuers free to spring up anywhere, money would be "made" anywhere.

There was, of course, the risk that the new money issuers could make poor decisions. If they seeded new businesses with new money and the businesses failed, the economy would have no more real supply than before, while a bunch of new notes with claims on precious metals were circulating. At some point, the notes would find themselves back at the place of issue, and the stock of precious metals would not be large enough to clear the reacceptance of the notes. The bank bailouts of our own day cut or eliminate these classic feedback loops. In contemporary times, supervisory and "too big to fail" institutions block or suppress communication of financial information in ways unknown in the era of note-issuance on the basis of a specie standard.

If, on the other hand, the note-issuers were unscrupulous profiteers, they could take advantage of the excitement generated by the burst of entrepreneurialism and lend currency redeemable in precious metals without respect to good business cause. There would not be much sense in doing this, however, in that the only value an issuer would get in return was the interest payment. If the businesses lent to were poor in the first place, such payments would not be made, and the note-issuer would see no profit. Thus, there was little incentive even for the corrupt to pursue such a course of action.

The modern system, in dubious contrast, in lacking a feedback loop system sufficiently in place, has more difficulty preventing bad loans for political, opportunistic, or unscrupulous reasons. A key to a good system is not having altruistic people in place who overcome incentives to do the right thing. Rather, it is having incentives and structures that direct potentially unvirtuous people to do the right thing. To be sure, virtue is essential for the proper functioning of business, government, and society, as the American founders amply recognized. But to have a system—it is fair to speak of today's in this way—in which people are to do what the system encourages them not to do is backward.

Prior to the American Revolution, North American colony governments issued paper currency. There were few, if any, mining operations, and the place needed money. Gold and silver coin came in via foreign commerce, but it was not enough to finance an economy bent on improvement and expansion. Colonial governments, increasingly in concert with local businesspeople, printed money on the basis of assets such as land and tobacco, as well as on claims on future tax revenue. They also pooled mortgages and let the mortgage notes circulate as currency. A standard division obtained whereby for local transactions, people used local paper money, and for international transactions they used foreign coin. Generally, the money, denominated in the English system of pounds, shillings, and pence, traded at a modest discount to the similar denominations of gold and silver coin. What the paper currency could buy at a given denomination was a little less compared to what coin could buy.

The inestimable monetary historian Richard Sylla wrote of this era:

> One would be hard pressed to find a place and time in which there was more monetary innovation than in the British North American colonies in the century and a half before the American Revolution....
>
> Why did all of this monetary innovation take place on a periphery far removed from the heart of western civilization?....
>
> The British North American colonies in all likelihood were the most rapidly growing economy in the world of the seventeenth and eighteenth centuries....
>
> The colonial American economy...was decidedly modern in its overall rate of economic growth. The traditional moneys, gold and silver, were either unavailable or available in insufficient amounts to sustain this growth, and more generally, colonial economic development. The innovation of new forms of money was the solution to a persistent problem of colonial life.

The Stamp Act of 1765 mandated payment in hard British money across a variety of colonial sales of goods. It incurred the ire of the colonists for good reason. The colonists had been economizing on money because their economy was growing so much. They could not afford to blow precious gold or silver on British "stamps" to enable the publication of a newspaper, for example, because money had become so valuable in financing economic growth. The monetary dynamics of the Industrial

Revolution were blooming into full flower in the colonial period of American history. If the growth environment is great, there will have to be more currency and money than available through gold and silver alone.[11]

Monetary innovation is, therefore, a characteristic of economies in the midst of, or on the cusp of, a great wave of growth. The very emergence of Bitcoin and cryptocurrency in our own times is perhaps a herald that these times, our times, are also at the cusp of an era of great growth. Conditions for decades now in the United States, and in much of the advanced world as well, have not been suggestive of such a future. Since Bitcoin has in fact now emerged, if monetary innovation is awakening after a sleep of a century, is this not an indication of a mass yearning for great growth like we used to enjoy in the past? Bitcoin is monetary innovation, and monetary innovation enables and accompanies great real economic growth. Therefore, letting Bitcoin and cryptocurrency have their space and freedom is probably one of the best things we can do to let real economic growth emerge and flourish.

In the federal Constitution of 1789, if states wanted to declare a money medium a legal "Tender in Payment of Debts," as the colonies had before the Revolution, states had to make that medium "gold and silver Coin." The era of state paper money was over. It mattered little because colonial and post-1776 state governments had increasingly ceded monetary innovation functions to private institutions—banks, in a word. This constitutional tradition, the monetary law of the United States, is that which we surely should strive to adhere to today.

---

[11] Richard Sylla, "Monetary Innovation in America," *Journal of Economic History* [hereafter *JEH*] 42, no. 1 (March 1982), 23–24.

Anything counter, perhaps even the Federal Reserve, should be suggestive of illegality.

In the latter eighteenth century, as private issuers took over money-issuance functions from the states, alternative definitions of money, from claims on a portion of land or tobacco or even government revenue, fell away in favor of gold and silver. Owing to robust commerce, precious metal coin was flowing into American ports by the end of the 1700s, but again, this was not wholly necessary. A growing economy needs only a small minimum of gold and silver, because monetary instruments defined as redeemable in gold or silver, as opposed to gold and silver itself, will be the preference of currency holders when profitable opportunities are beckoning from every corner.

In the ideal, and increasingly in practice as the Industrial Revolution was first gathering steam, private entities issued paper money redeemable in a hard asset, typically weights of precious metals. This was a natural outcome of the definition of money. As the term "dollar" became popular in the eighteenth century (its origins are Bohemian), twenty dollars meant an ounce of gold. If a piece of paper currency said twenty dollars, it meant that the bearer could get an ounce of gold for it from the issuer.

Redeemability provided invaluable economic information to the institutions that were issuing the currency. The more people showed up to redeem the notes, the more it became clear, to the issuer, that perhaps not so much capital was really needed out there. The less people presented themselves with redemption requests, the greater the indication was that there was an appetite for more note-issuance. Perhaps a government currency-issuer could ignore such indications because it could force people to use its money. Private currency-issuers could not ignore the signals.

The expositor of supply-side economics Jude Wanniski put it this way in 2001, citing the wisdom of the first secretary of the Treasury, Alexander Hamilton: "With gold, [Hamilton] said, the bank always knows when it is printing one dollar too many, because it will show up somewhere in the economy and the person holding it will come to the bank and ask for gold. That little-bitty signal is all the [bank] needs to know at the end of the business day. If there is nobody at the gold window with surplus dollars and nobody at the dollar window with surplus gold, you know you are perfect in your management of the dollar." Here was the feedback loop in practice.[12]

This was another aspect of "monetary policy" in this world. The definition of currencies in precious metals provided on-the-spot information about how much people really wanted them. The correspondence with economic growth was assured. If the new currency issuance was assisting in increasing real economic supply, contributing to the great growth of the Industrial Revolution, people would not redeem the currency for gold to any significant degree. If there was new desirable stuff to buy, the chance people would buy gold as opposed to this new stuff was naturally small. If there was not new stuff that people wished to buy—if the new business ideas had turned out to be bad ones—the banks would find out soon enough when people came to turn the currency notes in for precious metals.

The pertinent economic term is "opportunity cost," or the cost of what one is doing as opposed to an alternative. The proper goal of a currency is to have the opportunity cost of

---

12 Jude Wanniski, "T.J. Rodgers, Man on the Margin," polyconomics.com, April 11, 2001, at www.wanniski.net/memos/mm-010411.htm.

holding the base money (gold or silver classically) so high that people, without instruction or official prodding, would prefer to transact in and hold currency over the monetary base of that currency.

Bitcoin and history

We know, of course, that the Industrial Revolution succeeded. There most certainly was more great stuff to buy once entrepreneurs got their hands on capital. Therefore, the experiment in issuing paper money redeemable in precious metals also succeeded.

The experiment arose organically, and it attended the greatest development in economic history and human prospering over all the millennia. And it is now relegated to the past. Today, paper money has no redemption feature into precious metals, which themselves play no part in the definition of money. Yet if we aspire to great economic growth—as surely we do—we should maintain an interest in the monetary system of the great days of the Industrial Revolution. If the monetary secret of those days became our secret today, we would have reason to believe that a new long season of flush economic success and expansion could be our fate as well.

Bitcoin has characteristics uncannily similar to gold. It is fixed in supply. The next unit is more difficult to get than the last (this is essential to a store of value because the difficulty represents the storing of time—the time to create the next unit). It is clunky as a transaction medium. It has aboriginal, cult-like appeal. Its advocates insist that it is money, no matter any objection. It comes into existence by "mining" on the part of anyone who wants to get it in that fashion. All of these things are like gold. Other cryptocurrencies, Ether for example, are perhaps like silver. While still limited in supply, they are prospectively more abundant and easier to use as a transaction medium. They are followers of Bitcoin, of "gold," the little sisters and brothers. They have all, with Bitcoin, arisen after a long season of popular exasperation with fiat money and a yearning for large, American Dream-style economic growth.

When the Industrial Revolution was in its formative stages, natural processes, often associated with discussions of the matter in the realm of public affairs, hit on how the monetary system should be organized in the event of economic growth. Still, action predominated over theory, talk, and writing. Opportunities beckoned, giving primacy to doing over deliberation. People assumed that precious metals—gold and silver above all—were the money that one knew others would accept in exchange. But it was also quickly grasped that given economic growth, money would have to expand to meet the increase in goods and services. Here arose currency that was redeemable in precious metals.

Since Bitcoin's creation in the 2008 white paper and the first transactions of 2009, it is almost as if a process of "recapitulation" has begun to occur. It is as if the monetary consciousness of the world has been striving to rediscover, to reclaim, how money had been done when the world really got rich for the first time in modern history, at the dawn of the Industrial Revolution. Back then, in the eighteenth century, Newton had his experiments, and the likes of Franklin (and Adam Smith and David Hume and a number of others) presented their useful views to the public. The priority, however, was not on elaborating a monetary scheme so much as getting a very important task done. The Industrial Revolution was dawning, and people needed good money to make it happen. So people made good money happen, whatever the natural constraints of the production of precious metals.

Franklin himself in later years would become, as best we can estimate it, the richest individual in the country. If he was a theorist of money, it was in part because he had an eye on tremendous opportunities beckoning in the "real world." His fortune, it turned out, largely came, initially, from selling printed sermons from Great Awakening circuit preachers. A society experiencing economic growth led to free time to attend tent meetings; an interest in perfecting one's life in the context of growing abundance; and spending money on things that are not food, clothing, and shelter, including sermons. Franklin saw economic growth as a prospective permanent condition, chipped in with some ideas about money, and then got involved in the great growth.

The sequence today is different in important respects. Legendary economic growth is the legacy of the past, of the generations that preceded the contemporary ones. To Franklin, legendary economic growth was not part of the past. Rather, it was nigh in the future. In the eighteenth century, the challenge was to create the money system of an economy that yearned, that was primed to grow. In the twenty-first century, the challenge is to recapture the ways of growth. Therefore, attention has turned, if indirectly and in a way appropriate to contemporary conditions, toward a rediscovery of the monetary system that enabled the legendary growth of past eras. Attention has turned toward recreating the kind of money that stored the value of time, given that when we use our time productively today, we are so very productive.

It is a powerful sign that Bitcoin and cryptos appear to be recapitulating the monetary history of earlier foundational economic epochs. In biology, recapitulation theory expresses how organisms develop and equip themselves to function in the current environment. In its gestation, in this theory, an organism goes through the various stages of development of the previous forms of that organism, even ones that have died out due to their lack of adaptability as circumstances changed. It appears that it may be useful for an organism to experience the developmental stages of its forebears that functioned in older environments when organizing itself to be functional in a new environment.

Philosophers as far back as Friedrich Schelling in the nineteenth century have noted the applicability of the biological concept of recapitulation to social systems. In Schelling's "nature philosophy," the patterns that organize the life of plants and animals have their impress on human affairs as well. Bitcoin and cryptos have markers of the "collective unconscious" (the concept of Jung's), a pan-personal form of harmonized apperception common to humanity that links habits of thought and action across time. Bitcoin's emulation of gold; the prospect that Bitcoin presents as a potential alternative store of value; the various cryptos arising to serve as useful money on the inspiration of the leader; the primordial thrill and practical determination of the crypto community in spurring on crypto innovation—all are strong suggestions that this new money is emerging from an archetype (a Jungian term) in human consciousness and history.

Such notions need not remain speculative or fuzzy. The rise of Bitcoin and allied cryptocurrencies is calling forth a necessary historical reassessment—a relearning. The monetary history of the greatest economy ever in the world, that of the

United States, is consistent with the emerging monetary system suggested by Bitcoin and crypto. Indeed, absorbing that history confers a familiarity with and understanding of the outlines of the Bitcoin phenomenon. A reason that Bitcoin and its epigones in crypto might appear weird and offbeat to many of us (cars were weird in the 1890s, as novelist Booth Tarkington wrote about) is the disappointing one that we may have incorrect impressions of our own monetary history.

The general outlines of eighteenth-century monetary history in the emerging United States, and those of Newton's labors in math and at the British mint, should make us comfortable with the idea that the world toward which Bitcoin monetary innovation is beckoning has a precedent. As the American colonies participated, at a remove, in the early stages of the Industrial Revolution in Britain, primed for take-off, it became apparent that the place needed more money. It was also apparent that while governments could possibly handle the task of the issuance of new money, competitive private entities were the best at it. In the nineteenth century, as the United States embarked on its own growth at impressive rates, these realizations took on ever greater clarity and practical application.

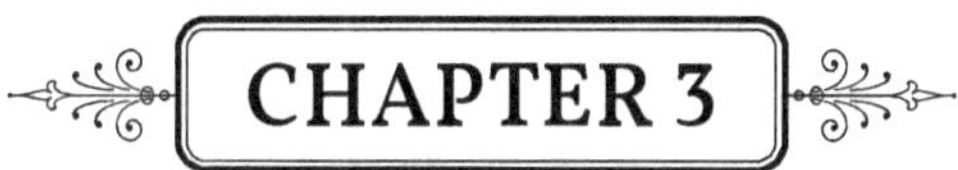

CHAPTER 3

The American Way of Currency

When the United States broke away from Great Britain in 1776, it was a country of 2.5 million persons. Over the next decades, the population kept growing and growing. On the eve of the Civil War in 1860, the country had thirty-one million inhabitants, and by 1900, seventy-six million. Over the first century and a quarter of the nation's existence, the population grew twenty-five-fold. The boundaries of the country expanded too. In 1776, the United States was an Atlantic seaboard country. In 1900, it was a transcontinental one. In terms of economic growth, the expansion was at its most remarkable. On modern reconstructions, economic growth in the United States from 1790 to 1900 tallied a little over a hundredfold. It was epic.

The "size" of an economy is an abstraction. "Gross national product," the measure of the total amount of final goods and services produced in an economy in a given year, was first calculated systematically in the 1930s. Figures for the nineteenth century have come care of economic historians. The hundredfold increase in the size of the American economy in the 110 years prior to 1900 is one of the most stunning developments in all of history writ large. Here was a small society that became big and, as it did so, became productive and richer at about four times the rate of its major population growth.

The American products and services that emerged, or were substantially improved, in the nineteenth century make up a lengthy and breathtaking list, a cornucopia of new things. For starters, there was transportation. Goods and people gained the capacity to move across distance to a new and remarkable degree. Steamboats were a prime example. In 1815, there were seven steamboats on major American rivers across the vast Gulf of Mexico watershed. In 1855, there were 696. In 1855, these boats could travel at double or triple the speed of the boats of 1815. Passengers logged 5 million miles in 1815 and 2.6 billion miles in 1855. Goods shipped went from 5 million freight-miles to 3.8 billion. As steamboat travel reached these peaks, railroads came along and raised them to greater heights.[13]

As for the production of agricultural goods, they soared beyond all precedent. In the sixty years before 1900, corn harvested per year in the United States went from 378 million bushels to 2.7 billion. Wheat production went up eightfold. Every agricultural commodity of note increased in yield at similar rates. The jarring, canning, and refrigerated transport of food emerged wholesale. And food production had a limit. At some point, people stop eating and storing food—they have had enough.[14]

---

[13] *Historical Statistics of the United States: Millennial Edition*, eds. Susan B. Carter et al. (New York: Cambridge University Press, 2006), Series Df641–650.

[14] *Historical Statistics of the United States*, Series Da707–716, 730–732.

The production of non-agricultural goods and the pro-vision of services therefore increased at an even greater rate. Lighting in 1800 was largely a matter of expensive (and dangerous and malodorous) candles. By the 1850s, when Herman Melville wrote *Moby-Dick*, whale oil harvesting had brought a new means of illumination to thousands of buildings. By the 1880s, the Standard Oil Corporation, symbolized by its torch logo, was chiefly responsible for fueling indoor illumination in the houses, apartments, and office buildings that had come in immense numbers with the population and economic growth. Then came the adoption of Thomas Edison's electric light bulb.

Perhaps excepting only farm-engineering advances, housing was the most dramatic growth good in the United States during this period. In Kentucky, in 1809 (Honest Abe's birth year), Abraham Lincoln's family had probably been spending nights in a shelter like a lean-to. Such an abode was not uncommon on the American frontier in those days. By the end of the century, the burgeoning American population had experienced a renaissance in living quarters. Single-family houses, with a number of rooms and floors, and apartment buildings—like those houses networked for heating, water, and sewage when not electricity and communications (the telephone)—were completely unlike the average abode of the eras before.

As the historian Robert Gordon has noted, we modern people are apt to look down at the "tenement" housing of circa 1900 in America. In New York City, the term "tenement" meant a building with three or more housing units. "Popular images of housing in the late nineteenth century are heavily influenced by social reformers such as the Danish immigrant newspaper reporter Jacob Riis," as Gordon wrote in his epic history *The Rise and Fall of Economic Growth* (2016). "Riis's title, *How the*

Other Half Lives, greatly exaggerates the misery of the working class for the nation taken as a whole."

Gordon continued:

> The population more than tripled over the 1870–1940 interval, and the number of households grew almost fivefold....

> There was almost a complete turnover in the American housing stock from 1880 to 1940. Of the dwellings that existed in 1940, only 7.3 percent were built before 1880.

And quoting contemporary observer James Bryce in his 1888 book *The American Commonwealth*:

> In cities like Cleveland or Chicago...miles on miles of suburb filled with neat wooden houses, each with its tiny garden plot, owned by the shop assistants and handicraftsmen who return on the horse cars in the evening from their work....The impression which this comfort and plenty makes is heightened by the brilliance and keenness of the air, by the look of freshness and cleanness which even the cities wear. The fog and soot-flakes of the English town, as well as its squalor, are wanting: you are in a new world, and a world which knows the sun.

In metropolitan Chicago from 1910 to 1930, one hundred thousand bungalows beyond even the type Bryce described were built. And "the feasibility of...lawn areas surrounding houses," as Gordon observed, "was facilitated by the invention, in the 1860s, of the lightweight lawnmower."[15]

Vignettes such as these could go on and on and on. The range of American products that emerged over the course of the nineteenth century is indescribable. *The Rise and Fall of American Growth* devotes six hundred pages to the innumerable details of this era's growth, of all the new products and services. Mason jars, window screens, cornflakes, lawnmowers, cable cars, multitudes of detached homes, no more carrying water, burning down the house, or having your face disfigured with burns (the fate of poet Henry Wadsworth Longfellow) as a lamp or candle falls and lights up someone's dress (as it did to Mrs. Longfellow), or waiting outside for the privy—each one of these represents a chink through which we can see the immensity of new American production in the nineteenth century.

It was a case of Isaac Newton's exponential function. All the new stuff America produced greatly exceeded what the nation had produced before. And the process kept on going, year after year, whatever the odd panic or depression. It was a cumulative process of most heady economic growth, each success setting up more success later on. The integral under the exponential curve of American growth in the nineteenth century was a huge mass of economic product unlike anything before.

In the nineteenth century, material things, economic goods and services increased by a simply fantastic amount. Gold and silver did not. This would have been impossible. Steamboats did not continue to increase at an exponential rate. They did for a while, then the railroad came and did it better. Same thing

---

[15]   Robert J. Gordon, *The Rise and Fall of American Growth: The U.S. Standard of Living since the Civil War* (Princeton: Princeton University Press, 2016), 97, 99, 104, 108.

with candles and whale oil. They increased until electricity performed their function better and became moot.

There was no way that precious metal production could keep pace with the fantastic economic growth of the era of the Industrial Revolution. Therefore, there had to be innovations in money, just as there were with every other product. To be sure, gold and silver production picked up with the Industrial Revolution. The transportation and engineering advances made sure of it. Still, gold and silver output had no chance of keeping pace with the general rate of growth of the Industrial Revolution. No chance at all.

There were gold strikes, the most consequential prompting the California gold rush of 1849, itself impossible without the transportation revolution and the businesses of Cornelius Vanderbilt in particular. The Yukon and Klondike strikes of several decades later were comparable to the California strike, as was the Nevada Comstock silver lode bonanza. Globally, strikes in South Africa and the application of new industrial engineering techniques increased the available supply of precious metals. All told, the total world stock of the representative monetary metal, gold, went up about four times from 1800 to 1900. This works out to 1.4 percent per year. During the same period, American growth was fifty-seven-fold, 4.1 percent per year. Economic growth in Great Britain, Japan, Germany, France, and any number of other economies whose currency systems were based on metallic money was nearly as great and exceptional.[16]

This was the tally: over the years of the Industrial Revolution, the amount of stuff produced ludicrously exceeded new output

---

[16]   Turk, "The Aboveground Gold Stock: Its Importance and Size," 14.

of gold and silver. And all the while, the monetary system of the Industrial Revolution was one of gold and silver. This paradox is at once a means of comprehending the past and the key to monetary progress and reform in the twenty-first century.

The first American money system

The United States established the outlines of its monetary system before the prodigious advances of its Industrial Revolution began to take hold. This monetary system, made in the Revolutionary and Federal eras of American history, proved perfectly adaptable to the yet unseen Industrial Revolution leaps of the nineteenth and early twentieth centuries. This was so even though bank regulation made geographical diversification (common, for example, in Canada) impossible until, in the 1980s, the Supreme Court permitted a bank's far-flung Automated Teller Machines.

That the received, pre-industrial monetary system provided no bar to the Industrial Revolution—that it proved fully compatible with epochal economic transformation and development—is a fact of the first significance. Here was the monetary system that accompanied the Industrial Revolution from the beginning. Therefore, *ipso facto*, it was most remarkable, should be studied for the lessons it provides about history, and is a candidate for emulation in modern times.

"The thirteen united States of America," to quote the first phrase of the Declaration of Independence, had quite a bit of difficulty with respect to money as they broke away from Great Britain in 1776. Prior to the Revolutionary War, what gold and silver coins had been flowing throughout the American colonies, little of it had come from an American source. Coins struck in the West Indies, Latin America, Europe, and Asia made up the metallic monetary base of the American economy at the time of independence. Where it existed, paper money was issued by colonial authorities in concert with entrepreneurial citizens. This system, developed organically (as Bitcoin has developed organically), worked well. Production and commerce bloomed in the eighteenth century. It is a period we now see as the first part of the take-off of the Industrial Revolution.

Extended warfare is an activity, however, that typically changes the nature of the demand for money. Demand for the kind of money—currency—that can readily be used for investment and purchases wanes. Demand for the kind of money that comparatively serves well as a savings instrument—precious metals, for example—rises. The matter Jude Wanniski described in the 1990s applies. During warfare, people become less interested in holding currency and "notes" and seek to exchange them for gold and silver.

The United States got involved in a six-year war, the Revolutionary War, whose battles went on from 1775 to 1781. Since war is by nature destructive, it necessarily reduces wealth and, crucially, the average rate of return on investments in general. The "real" demand for money—the demand for money to be used in productive economic activity—falls during warfare. People who have paper money will return it to the issuer for metal at a greater rate than during a peacetime in which the market economy is operating normally.

This puts belligerents in a bind. They have a war to finance. One strategy they can call on is to issue paper currency, make it unredeemable at present in metal, and urge the population to use it out of a sense of patriotism and to support the war effort. The implication is that if the war is successful, there will be economic growth afterward, and the money created during the war can finance the peacetime boom when it comes.

This is nice in theory. In the pressing circumstances of war, the practicalities can be overwhelming. In the 1770s, the Continental Congress ended up issuing so much paper that tremendous inflation took hold. The Pennsylvania legislature countered by backing some of its currency in land, including a portion of western Pennsylvania north of Pittsburgh which George Washington and his associate Christopher Gist had superficially surveyed in the 1750s. To this day, properties along the old Perry Highway north of the Steel City are known as the "depreciation lands."

After the treaty with the British that assured the nation's independence in 1783, the American money system started to revert to its natural organic self. The increased economic activity that came with peace drew in gold and silver coin from sources foreign and domestic. The restoring of commerce, and investment returns with it, called money into circulation. People used their saved gold and silver for investments and purchases. New paper currency in the forms of letters of credit, and bank issuance, arose as well, a testament to the return of a good economy in peacetime.

The states, however, remained perplexed about the condition of their finances. They had borrowed much during the war years, and their plans for keeping up debt payments were lacking. States were tax-competitive with each other, even imposing tariffs against each other's goods. Raising tax rates was a sure way of driving away business and residents. A solution began to emerge: organize a new federal government, and have it pick up the state debts.

This was a central point of discussion at the constitutional convention of the summer of 1787. The delegates debated this issue among others, produced a document, and within a year, the requisite number of states had ratified the Constitution. It enabled the federal government to assume all state debts as its own singular debt. Congress acted on this power in 1790, and the state debts were gone, made into a unitary federal debt. This first national debt amounted to $70 million, which corresponded to perhaps 40 percent of yearly national economic output (compared to 100-plus percent today).

Having relieved the states of their debt burdens, the Constitution put limits on what the states could do monetarily under its authority. Article 1, Section 8, prohibited states from declaring as valid currency within their borders anything that was not "Gold and Silver Coin." The federal government alone—with uncertain constitutional authority, as the future would demonstrate—would reserve for itself the ability to declare whatever it wished as "legal tender for all debts, public and private," to quote from the top left front of our dollar bills today. Curiously, over the years, the federal government has specified that its currency is "legal tender" when that currency has either no link, or an attenuated link, to precious metals. When the dollar has been freely redeemable in gold or silver, it has been superfluous to say it is legal tender. People accept such currency readily. In the latter eighteenth century, when the United States said its coins were legal tender, it did so while providing that they were legal tender only to the degree that they had the metal they claimed to have.

The Constitution also specified that Congress had the power to "coin Money" and "regulate the Value thereof." By "coin Money," the federal body could strike coins, presumably from some precious metal. By "regulate the Value thereof," Congress could do two things. It could specify ratios among weights of different metals struck as coins. And it could assign monetary denominations to those coins respectful of those ratios.

In the Coinage Act of 1792, Congress established the United States Mint, specified silver as one-fifteenth the monetary value of gold, and declared a series of coin values that the Mint could strike. "Dollar" coins were to have 89 percent of an ounce of silver, plus an amalgam that kept the coin physically together. As the law put it, each silver United States dollar was "to be of the value of a Spanish milled dollar as the same is now current." The Spanish dollar—the term alluded to the place of origin of a similar German coin—had approximately the same amount of silver and circulated widely across the globe. The Coinage Act also authorized the Mint to strike a coin with a proportional amount of gold (given the one-to-fifteen ratio) and include silver as part of the bonding alloy. It would be specified as ten dollars and called an "eagle." For small change, the act provided for silver dimes, tenths of a dollar, and copper pennies.[17]

There was no necessary reason for the United States to go through all this and act on its power to strike coins. Coins produced the world over, such as the Spanish dollar, made their way into the American economy when it was in its peacetime productive mode. The reason the United States chose to strike coins in 1792 was competitive. The United States wanted users to choose its coins over other alternatives, so as to gain the United States some prestige and advertising and—crucially—to make a profit.

---

[17] *Coinage Act of 1792*, 2nd Congress, 1st Session, April 2, 1792.

The Coinage Act invited all comers with silver or gold bullion (*bullion*: from a French word for "boiled") to come to the Mint and "speedily" receive "free of expense" the equal value of coins struck from that bullion. Here was a service the Mint was offering free of charge. Precious-metal bullion does not function as a currency. The metal struck with the authentic marks of a reputable minter assures its owners and potential owners of its weight and authenticity. A silver dollar struck in this way has a high degree of credibility: that it is in fact an officially certified disc of 89 percent good silver. Today's fiat dollar has credibility as a transaction instrument, to be sure. It lacks credibility as a store of value. Few people leave their savings in cash. Instead, they take on risk and seek out interest-bearing instruments, bonds, stocks, real estate, and alternative investments. Bitcoin and cryptocurrency, whatever their price gyrations, suggest, aspirationally perhaps, a world in which, once again, there is a prospect of saving in cash.

The striking of coins is an economic service, an improvement to the bullion that adds value to it. It is interesting, therefore, that, at least initially, the United States did not charge for it. But that is the way of so many early-stage businesses: they give their product away so as to get people used to it and, perhaps in time, willing to pay for it. This is the business concept of a "loss leader." The Spanish charged a small fee for bullion depositors to get coins. Therefore, people could melt down Spanish dollars into bullion and get marginally more in dollar coins from the United States.

The Mint had expenses that made striking bullion for free a loss-making operation. The Coinage Act laid out at least $7,900 in yearly salaries that had to be paid to the Mint's executives, assayers, engravers, clerks, and "subordinate workmen and servants." There were capital and further operational expenses as well. Funds to pay for these things would have to come out of tax receipts—even though the Mint was literally making money.[18]

The act added, however, that if persons presenting bullion to the Mint so wished, they could walk away on the spot, without having to wait around for the striking and the engraving of their own bullion, with previously struck coin with precious metal makeup equal in weight to their bullion. There would be a half a percent charge for this service, for getting coins immediately. And with this, the Mint began to explore its profit-making promise. If people really liked American coins, they could bring their metal and get some right away, for a small fee.

These homely details of the original American monetary system are of the first importance in understanding the nascent monetary conditions of the twenty-first-century world, in which the monetary alternatives of cryptocurrencies bracingly present themselves as business propositions. Money-making, classically, was a profit-making activity. It may have been a public service, a public good, a duty and power of government, and so forth, but in addition it was done to make a profit.

The Spanish could charge for coining bullion because their coins were the preferred ones the world over. Everyone was willing to use and accept them. Therefore, to get one's bullion stamped as such, one had to pay a price. The United States noticed a competitive opportunity. It would strike coins for which the bullion provider waited for free, and it would charge a little less than the Spanish for immediate delivery. Either way, demand would flow to the United States and, along with it, the

---

[18] *Coinage Act of 1792*, Sec. 6.

beginnings of a profit stream. The Spanish might react and cut prices (in a word, a feedback loop). Then, the race would be on to see who the most efficient producer of money was. Who could strike a coin that retained its characteristics and attracted holders and users? This was (and is) the way of all business—quality control, marketing, advertising (as is inherent in the face of coins)—and it was central to the monetary business of the United States as it set up its coin system in the Federal period of history.

Not to have done this for profit would have ruined the whole activity. If the Mint coined bullion for free for the duration, undercutting the Spanish, bullion would have flowed to the United States. The Mint would have run up expenses accordingly, and taxes would have to be raised to pay for them. This would have worsened the investment climate in the United States because the rate of return of economic enterprises would decrease with tax increases. And in response, this would depress the demand for the nation's coins. It was more efficient to charge precisely at the point of sale rather than have the tax system sustain the Mint through the back door.

Conceivably, the Mint could have become so good at striking coins that it could have gobbled up global market share from the Spanish such that the federal government could cut taxes. If the Mint became supremely profitable, a virtuous circle would have been engaged. The Mint would strike many coins for a profit and turn over the profit to the Treasury. Congress would cut taxes. This would raise the rate of return of economic enterprises in the country, calling forth new investment and with it more money inclusive of the striking of coins. The Mint would reel in more profits as capital flowed into the United States and as the enterprises within it succeeded and grew.

This possibility is not far-fetched in the least. In modern times—at least since World War II—the United States dollar has been the inordinately preferred currency the world over. It has never been clear why the United States, since 1945, has had reason for a tax system, given that it can print money and have all the peoples of the globe hand over goods and services so as to be able to hold and use this money, the American dollar. If this idea sounds odd or even offensive to us, it is, at least in part, a testament to how much we have forgotten, or never gotten to know, about how monetary systems, including our own in its founding years, have classically worked. The tax system over the United States' time as a global hegemon has perhaps been little more than a mechanism of the government's to extract favors from the economy.

One reason—probably the active one—that the representatives and officials of the United States have for not eliminating the nation's tax system is that tax systems confer value to political activities. Lobbying for a tax reduction or exemption matters to people when tax rates are above modest levels. If the United States had taken the opportunity available to it, at least after 1945, to eliminate its tax system, Congress and the federal bureaucracy would have found itself more irrelevant. Important personages would not have been besieging them regularly for tax favors and breaks.

Two points remain imperative concerning the late eighteenth-century monetary system that the United States hammered out on digesting the reality of its independence. The first was that the making of money was not merely a public service. It was a business enterprise inseparable from the profit motive. The second concerns juxtaposition. In the late eighteenth century, it was just perceptible enough that in the nineteenth century, there was to be tremendous growth in goods and services—simply tremendous. The monetary system set up on the cusp of this new era was one of gold and silver, with the coinmaker having competitive and profit-making ambitions.

These historical realities were linked, the effect to its cause, in a way that can enlighten us as we consider new possibilities about money in our age today. The upcoming decades may well promise to be ones of tremendous economic growth. Space travel and exploration, the return of mass small-scale farming assisted by technology, fantastic virtual experiences—investors and developers are working on bringing such epochal things into existence. It would be odd, in an economy characterized by creativity, for the monetary system itself not to participate in some fundamental way with creativity. The proposition that mainstay twentieth-century bureaucracies, such as the Federal Reserve or the International Monetary Fund or the legacy big banks, will sponsor monetary creativity is obviously unsound. Legacy corporations did not discover the new applications of the internet. Start-ups did. After the development of the transistor in 1947, Bell Labs in New Jersey was notable more for its interesting architecture and the volume of its employment rolls (upwards of fifteen thousand) than its occasional fundamental discovery.

Start-ups in the monetary space—this is consistent with the tenor of the times. Bitcoin in particular, however, is no mere start-up. It is, to be sure, a breakthrough product of mysterious unknown provenance that is taking advantage of the global ubiquity of the internet. But it is also a start-up that draws from historical experience, from a monetary status quo of previous times. One excellent reason to see staying power in Bitcoin is that coupled with its bona fides as a technological and internet phenomenon, it is a vehicle for recovering, in monetary affairs, the vibrancy of the past that somehow went lost in modern times. To be hard-headed about it, private money went by the boards in modern times surely because political authorities saw in it a diffusion of power across society that was not entirely to their taste.

Preparing the take-off

In the 1790s, the American economy started along the big growth trajectory it would sustain for decades upon end. By modern reconstructions, economic growth was 6 percent per year from 1790 to 1800 and just under 4 percent from 1800 to 1810, the latter portion afflicted by Napoleon's military campaigns over land and sea. New products and services—and with them, profits and investments—were coming on strong.

The national debt went down accordingly. By 1810, it had sunk to $53 million from the initial $71 million of 1790. In terms of the size of the economy, and therefore the ability of the government-receipts system to service the debt, in 1810 the debt over twenty years had been reduced by about 80 percent. Moreover, the nation's population had nearly doubled in the interval. Per capita, the debt in 1810 was 60 percent less than in 1790.

The United States serviced this debt mainly through tariff revenue. This had not necessarily been the plan. There is a tendency in American history to overplay the first secretary of the Treasury Alexander Hamilton's 1791 *Report on Manufactures* as the "plan" for the American economy under the Constitution. Hamilton's *Report* called for domestic industries to spring up under the protection of a tariff and the subsidies to those industries that customs duties could finance. The United States initiated a tariff, to be sure, as the second law of the land (the first concerned oaths of office) on July 4, 1789. But it was not supposed to carry the load of the tax system. There were also supposed to be all sorts of domestic taxes at the federal level.

These indeed came in the 1790s. It quickly became apparent that domestic taxation would not work. The most notorious case was the federal whiskey tax. It inspired such revulsion and mockery that tax collectors not far from the depreciation lands in western Pennsylvania found themselves tarred and feathered when they tried to collect it. President George Washington sent troops to put down this rebellion in 1794. The lesson of the episode was clear. It would be better to relieve the domestic population of taxation as much as possible because that population was ornery about taxation. The tariff, in contrast, was paid by foreigners. And they had to pay it, or agree to pay it, shortly after they landed at an American port, at the custom house right there on shore. If they declined, they would be shown the port's siege guns.

Thus, the tariff became the chief means of federal tax revenue in these years. Congress kept the tariff going while paring away various excise taxes paid directly by the nation's inhabitants. By 1806, customs revenue had grown fourfold since the early 1790s as "internal revenue" from domestic sources went to nil.[19]

The highly voluntary nature of tariff-duty payments was crucial to the conception and functioning of the system, as voluntarism is central to any well-functioning feedback loop. The tariff voluntarism had a counterpart in the monetary system

---

[19]   *Historical Statistics of the United States*, Series Ea588–593.

that was just as crucial in that realm. Merchants seeking to ship goods across the ocean into the United States knew that they had to commit to paying customs on their wares as soon as they landed, well before they unloaded their goods and sold them. The financial challenge of such an operation was formidable. Not only did the goods have to be produced, brought to the foreign port, and loaded on the merchant vessel filled with wage-laboring workers. At the conclusion of the outward journey, the customs bill had to be paid or at least guaranteed. All this required considerable upfront financing. This financing would not be forthcoming unless there was a clear sense that a nice profit was to be made after all the transactions cleared.

Congress, therefore, had to be careful to design the tariff such that its rates were not so high as to discourage importation. If Congress cared about revenue—which it did given the assumption of state debts after 1789, let alone the Whiskey Rebellion—it had to collect intimate knowledge about the profit margins of imported goods and be sure to tack on a tariff duty that did not, in the main, take these margins too low or make them negative. If tariff duties did go that high, merchants across the sea would not think of obtaining financing to bring goods across to the American market. Respecting the detailed profit ambitions of foreign merchants was essential to the success of the tariff as a revenue device. Congress respected the feedback loops of the tariff, of the "Laffer curve" effects, which we shall treat in the next chapter, of sometimes being able to lower a tax rate so as to bring in more revenue.

Congress had to be just as careful in its making of money. People had to volunteer to accept it. If those who brought bullion to the Mint had to pay a high fee to get it coined, they would not bring it. If the Mint lowered the precious metal content of the coins, people would demand a discount. If Congress mandated its money had to be accepted at face value "for all debts, public and private," it would have to enforce the mandate throughout a big and growing country, itself an expense that would drain the Treasury, require tax increases, and decrease the demand for American coin. In both its main fiscal and monetary operations, the early American federal government had to indulge the economic preferences of the people at large.

When the United States was still a fledgling place setting out on the path of becoming a legendarily affluent society, it was careful to be receptive to the feedback loops of its systems of taxation and money. If taxes were too high in any instance, people would run away from any activity that incurred them. Congress took note and adjusted rates accordingly. If government coin was not a good monetary deal for both customer and issuer alike, either sales would dry up or taxes would be raised, ruining the whole thing. The United States respected the discrete information it obtained in setting tax and money policy. If it did not, business would depart, and the dispensable place might be left impoverished.

Perhaps we might counter that all this prevailed when the United States was a brave new country in supplication to the rest of the world. It was not a superpower, a "hyperpower," as the French have said, as it has been in the contemporary era. Hegemonic governments can call the shots: our money is legal tender, and that is that. All this, however applicable it may be today, does not account for one imperative historical reality: that prodigious economic growth, that of the nineteenth and early twentieth centuries, followed upon the United States' setting up a fiscal and monetary system in a notably modest and respectful-of-others fashion.

Notably, Bitcoin and cryptocurrency offer a glimpse of the way the United States used to do things when it had little other choice than to try to be competitive as it set up tax and monetary systems. If you transact in Bitcoin, someone makes a profit on it, namely the mining fees. This is explicit. Bitcoin's alternatives and competitors see the price structure and try to be competitive against it. All the while, information is flowing, informing Bitcoin miners and Bitcoin competitors alike what the global market for these devices prefers.

The United States acted this same way with respect to its tax and monetary systems when it was about to grow in the Federal period. In the contemporary age, it offers its money in a different fashion. It offers its dollars as a public service, sees doing so as its exclusive sovereign domain, and does it all on the counsel of elaborately credentialed professionals at the Federal Reserve. This is a completely different model from that which the country followed as it got started more than two centuries ago.

The era of professional, sovereign, non-explicitly profit-making, non-precious-metal money has been that since 1971 and the final dropping of the dollar link to gold. This final move severed any remaining ordinary market-based feedback loop regarding the demand for the dollar, replacing it with political norms in the banking regulation system and the academic aura of the Federal Reserve. This era since 1971 has been one of distinctly slower economic growth than the norm. The slow growth has been particularly chronic in the twenty-first century. Long-term growth rates have barely held at even 2 percent per year since 2000.

When money was explicitly profitable and offered to the public as an option among others, as at the cusp of the nineteenth century, a tremendous economic boom stood on the horizon. When money has been professional, sovereign, scholarly, and a public service, explanations have welled up about why the growth has come in so poor. Economic inequality, secular stagnation, and sufficiency of growth after a long industrial and technological revolution are common explanatory-exculpatory devices. Bitcoin and cryptocurrencies set aside such arguments by offering a viable, not merely money alternative but monetary-system alternative that, in essential respects, is similar to that which prevailed when in fact the United States was about to grow like gangbusters at the outset of its history. Therefore, the emergence of Bitcoin and cryptocurrency may well herald a future like that which came with the emergence of the first American monetary system of gold, silver, profit-making, feedback loops, and respect for the customer: one of abundant economic growth.

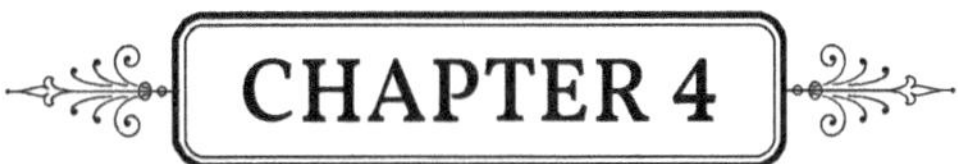

CHAPTER 4

Antebellum Alternatives:
A United States Bank
or Free Banking

The Federal Reserve had a predecessor. These were the two Banks of the United States, which existed in two twenty-year terms over the period 1791–1836. If the public looks askance at the Federal Reserve today, if it makes fun of its chairs for talking inscrutably, in gobbledygook, this is consistent with the skepticism with which the public regarded if not the first, then most certainly the second Bank of the United States, the one that lasted until 1836.

Popular unease with something resembling a central bank is a mainstay in the American experience, a *leitmotif* over several centuries of history. In the nineteenth century, this unease took the form of escorting the second bank out of existence against the wishes of its officers and congressional supporters, so as to make way for a system approximating the free private production of money. In the twenty-first century, this unease appears to be taking the form of Bitcoin and cryptocurrency's outlining and implementation of a completely alternative and private global monetary system. "Don't fight the Fed" is an adage in the financial markets. If the Fed is loosening or tightening, buy stock in complementary fashion. One might just as well say, "Don't fight opinion in a democracy." If the public has consistently wanted money to be private and is skeptical of government central banks, over hundreds of years, why not give in?

In 1791, Congress chartered the first Bank of the United States for a twenty-year term. The federal government owned a portion of its stock and had certain powers of appointment. This Bank of the United States was permitted, by congressional statute, to have branches in every state and be the place where one could pay federal taxes. The bank could accept deposits, make loans, and issue "notes" (or currency), which is to say, run the gamut of banking business.

The Bank of the United States was another one of Hamilton's ideas. It incurred opposition, mainly on the worry that it would breed cronyism. It became a football in the Federalist-Jeffersonian feud. It came into existence despite the opposition, gaining President Washington's signature on a congressional bill that passed comfortably, probably because of one clinching characteristic: its tax-collecting function. There were domestic taxes, and they had to be paid somewhere. There was no "Internal Revenue Service" or anything of the sort under the first Treasury. If whiskey or excise or capitation or whatever domestic taxes had to be paid by local inhabitants, a branch of the Bank of the United States, of which there were fourteen across the country, was the place to pay. This was a function of the Bank of the United States that no other bank could fulfill.

The Bank of the United States introduced an element of instability to the banking system of the fledgling country. The bank had a claim on domestic tax revenues and, thus, the deposits of the United States Treasury. The chance that it would fail was small. Necessarily, people preferred to keep their deposits in this bank. Other banks had to jack up interest rates to attract deposits. This led to a chasing of returns on the part of banks, taking flyers on the odd wild idea with loan money, and thus more frequent impairment and episodes of failure. The Bank of the United States was a self-fulfilling prophecy. If, as its proponents suggested, it was needed to provide the American banking system with an exemplar of stability, its existence ensured greater instability because of the risk of failure among institutions competing with it.

Within about ten years, the bank started to lose its claim on existence. The United States curtailed domestic taxation. After the distilled spirits tax of the early 1790s, Congress tried a land and property tax in 1798. It provoked another rebellion, the Fries Rebellion, smaller than the Whiskey Rebellion and again in Pennsylvania. After the United States Navy was able to clear the shipping routes of pirates in the Barbary Wars care of this tax's revenue, domestic taxation quickly came to nil as the tariff carried the federal government's revenue load. The *raison d'être* of the bank was melting away. There were few domestic taxes to pay. Tariff duties could be paid not at the interior banks but right there on shore, at the custom house. The bank's term expired in 1811, it folded, and its assets were taken into private hands.

All the while, during the first years of the Mint and the two-decade term of the Bank of the United States, the economy was growing. This meant that there was a demand for money surely greater than these two institutions could provide. As the American Numismatic Society has spoken of this era, "Coinage…was wholly inadequate for financing growth. With ever-growing needs for a medium of exchange, numerous banks and other businesses issued quantities of their own paper currency." In 1963, monetary historians Milton Friedman and Anna Schwartz estimated that paper money in circulation in the United States from 1790 to 1810 grew at least tenfold from an initial base of $2.5 million to $28 million. Bank of the United States issues averaged about a third of this paper currency. Private banks accounted for the rest. This paper money was in addition to circulating coin, which increased from $9 million to over $30 million in these years.[20]

The banking historian Bray Hammond wrote in 1957:

> In 1791, when the Bank of the United States was chartered,…there were three banks in operation. In 1811, when the Bank of the United States was let die,…banks…had multiplied from three to ninety. In the next five years the number increased to nearly 250; by 1820, it exceeded 300—an increase of more than a hundred-fold in the first years of the federal union.

Hammond reflected on this development:

> This growth was not the multiplication of something familiar, like houses or ships or

---

[20] "A History of American Currency," American Numismatic Society, at numismatics.org/a-history-of-american-currency; *Historical Statistics of the United States*, Series Cj7–21.

carriages, but a multiplication of something unfamiliar or even mysterious. Had banks been thought to be merely depositories where savings were tucked away—as came to be thought in time—there would have been nothing remarkable about their increase. But they were known to do more than receive money. They were known to create it. For each dollar paid in by the stockholders, the banks lent two, three, four, or five.

Something mysterious was taking hold in the country. The arrival of permanently large economic growth, via the first phases of the Industrial Revolution, was separating the monetary needs of the economy from the hard money stock. The exponential curve was starting on its course. The gap between that curve of great economic growth and the merely arithmetic increase in monetary metals had emerged. The new banks filled the gap with a new useful product. This was privately produced, profitably sold currency redeemable on demand on the government's definition in precious metals. There was precisely enough money to fund all the economic growth, a decreasing proportion of it was hard money, but the new currency was convertible on request of a holder into hard money.[21]

The expansion of banking—and thus currency issuance—over the first twenty years of American history of the Constitutional era happened, it must be stressed, while the first Bank of the United States was in existence and itself doing

---

[21] Bray Hammond, *Banks and Politics in America: From the Revolution to the Civil War* (Princeton: Princeton University Press, 1957), 145–46. By way of comparison, prior to the financial crisis of 2008, one dollar in mortgage bonds could be found basing nearly thirty dollars in loan amounts.

well. The bank turned out to be rather quick to learn that it should not seek to dominate the situation. Rather, it let other institutions explore the range of financial possibilities in the burgeoning American economy as the nineteenth century got underway. As the monetary historian Richard H. Timberlake observed of the first Bank of the United States:

> The dividends it paid were somewhat more modest than those of competing commercial banks, and the market value of its stock showed at best no appreciation even before its recharter became an issue. Meanwhile, the market values of its competitors' stocks increased considerably.

In 1811, the bank's gold and silver coin:

> reserve…was 37 percent of its outstanding demand obligations and almost 50 percent of its capital and surplus. It might therefore have generated considerably more demand and credit obligations than it actually did.

One might say that this bank artificially restricted the operation of natural feedback loops—it was too conservative, so as to maintain its image for probity and ward off accusations that it was political, all of this amounting to an economic deadweight loss. To speak like Aristotle, banks are best when fully functional as banks. The Bank of the United States, at least in the latter half of its twenty-year run until 1811, came to see that it was a threat to the stability of the financial system if it pressed its advantages. It therefore chose not to. Private currency issuance, in notes redeemable in gold or silver, increased magnificently as yearly 4–6 percent economic growth was financed without any general inflation or change in the spot price of monetary metals. It was an example of what gold-standard guru Nathan K. Lewis has called the "magic formula": low, voluntary tax rates and stable money, in this case largely private money redeemable in gold or silver, functioned as the fiscal and monetary policy of the first great era of American economic growth.[22]

Lady Antebellum

The early promising era of American financial and economic history ended with a thud with the War of 1812, which lasted until 1815. Warfare, as always, reduces the immediate return on investments in general and decreases the real demand for money. In particular, it leads to a "portfolio preference" on the part of money-holders and investors in favor of gold and silver over currency and financial paper. Since warfare is destructive, the demand for extra currency to finance new economic initiatives dries up. The growth in private currency outstanding through 1815, and especially federal note-issuance from 1812 to 1815, led to payment suspensions on the part of the issuers and nominal price inflation. In the nineteenth century, the term "broken bank notes" referred to currencies denominated as dollars that were supposed to be redeemable in gold or silver but could not be honored as such because of a rush at the redemption window.

The United States Treasury was in no enviable position during the War of 1812. People preferred gold and silver, not

---

[22] Richard H. Timberlake, *Monetary Policy in the United States: An Intellectual and Institutional History* (Chicago: University of Chicago Press, 1993), 9; Nathan Lewis, *The Magic Formula* (New Berlin, NY: Canyon Maple Publishing, 2019).

notes, because of the war, but the United States had the military to finance against a major power, Great Britain. Therefore the federal government took special measures. One was to introduce a currency that paid interest, about 5 percent. The thinking was that since gold and silver technically have a negative return rate—they pay no interest and incur storage and security expenses—this currency could budge the portfolio preference in its favor. Great Britain, for its part, suspended convertibility into gold for the duration of the long Napoleonic and French wars and had to resort to the novel device of income taxation because of diminished interest in the pound sterling. Former Chancellor of the Exchequer Kwasi Kwarteng has written a stirring book on such subjects in *War and Gold* (2014).

The United States got through the war with a victory in 1815 and a vast amount of currency and debts outstanding. Gold and silver had decamped for hoarding in private hands. With the proper peacetime reorientation, the currency system could rediscover its footing. An increase in the return rate on investments, on account of both peace itself and the norm of small peacetime taxation, would bring the gold and silver to market in exchange for currency that could be readily used for investment and transactions.

This happened—almost. By 1817, the federal government had eliminated all internal taxation (taxation on domestic inhabitants or transactions), a remarkable feat that held until 1861. In exchange, Congress and the president opted for a more extensive tariff than had prevailed to date. In addition, in 1816, Congress and the president rechartered a second Bank of the United States, again for a twenty-year term. As for the new tariff, it was somewhat punitive. Certain duty rates within it were explicitly excessive, or "prohibitive" or "protective" in the language of the day. In these cases, customs revenue from the given import would have been higher if the duty rate had been lower. This was so because importers would have brought in the taxed good in question in much larger quantities if the rate had gone down. Today, this general concept goes by the name the Laffer curve, after economist Arthur Laffer. In 1974, Laffer sketched a curve on a napkin before governmental officials, showing that tax rates can be so high that tax-rate cuts result in greater revenues.[23]

In the congressional debates in the nineteenth century, whether a tariff was "prohibitive," "protective," or "for revenue" were standard habits of speech. It is reasonable to say that given the tariff's primacy in the tax system of the period—it was the only federal tax from 1817 to 1861—the Laffer curve, as we call it today, was the organizing principle of American political economy, as it was discussed within the halls of Congress. By 1821, three-quarters of imports by dollar value were subject to duty rates. Over the next dozen years, these rates averaged between just under 40 percent and just over 60 percent. These tax rates were not low. But they were confined to the highly voluntary realm of international trade. If people did not want to pay them, they were free not to bring their goods into the United States.[24]

The absence of domestic taxation—the trade-off benefit of having the big tariff—brought about a surge in investment

---

[23] Brian Domitrovic, *The Emergence of Arthur Laffer: The Foundations of Supply-Side Economics in Chicago and Washington, 1966–1976* (Cham, Switzerland: Palgrave Macmillan, 2021), Ch. 8. Also see Laffer, "Reinstatement of the Dollar: The Blueprint," in Ch. 1 of *The Pillars of Reaganomics: A Generation of Wisdom from Arthur Laffer and the Supply-Side Revolutionaries*, ed. Brian Domitrovic (San Francisco: Pacific Research Institute, 2014).

[24] *Historical Statistics of the United States*, Series Ee424–430.

and economic activity. To be sure, the tariff made capital goods more expensive, and workers had to be paid more in the United States so that they could afford the goods jacked up in price by the tariff. But that was it. Aside from the tariff, there was no federal taxation providing a bar to entrepreneurial activity.

Why Congress chartered the second Bank of the United States is a fair question. If there was to be no domestic taxation, what was the point of the bank? The custom houses at the ports were sufficient to collect all federal taxes. It was never clear what the purpose of this second bank was. This was one of the reasons a lawsuit was brought challenging its legitimacy, the famous *McCulloch v. Maryland* Supreme Court case of 1819. Maryland tried to tax a branch of the bank in its state. Chief Justice John Marshall ruled in favor of the bank with his famous words, worthy of being put in boldface, "the power to tax involves the power to destroy," and confirmed that a state cannot tax a federal entity. Marshall added, oddly to Richard Timberlake, that the bank was constitutional on the grounds that the Constitution permitted Congress to make laws "necessary and proper" to carrying out its express powers. Reading the Tenth Amendment, Timberlake countered that "certainly, the power to incorporate *a bank* is one reserved to the states or the people." And if the bank was "necessary," then "how did the government manage without it between 1811 and 1816, and again between 1836 and 1914, when the Federal Reserve System began operations?"

The obvious dubiousness of the second Bank of the United States was one of the reasons the American economy did so well during its term and certainly after. As Timberlake noted of the bank after *McCulloch*:

During that time it thrived, carrying on its banking business with discretion and aplomb. How could it do otherwise with all the privileges and advantages it had over rival private institutions [including 20 percent federal ownership and thus a guarantee against failure from the Congress]? Always in the background, however, was the knowledge that its charter had a time limit, and would have to be renewed before 1836 if the Bank were to continue…. For this reason,…the Bank's directors were careful neither to claim or do too much.

This was shades of the latter period of the first Bank of the United States, in the decade prior to 1811, when the bank did not press its currency-issuance power and let other private institutions take that opportunity. Today, the non-time-limited explicit and implicit government guarantees to the financial sector lead to capital misallocation across industries and the negation of feedback loops, redounding to the power of politicians and the official bureaucracies.[25]

As the American economy grew magnificently in the decades after 1815, as the array of new products and services began to expand almost beyond description, privately issued currency redeemable in gold and silver came into its own as the financial medium that made the growth possible. A formidable example was that of Stephen Girard, a major Philadelphia farmer and merchant in the years prior to the War of 1812.

---

[25] Richard H. Timberlake, *Constitutional Money: A Review of the Supreme Court's Monetary Decisions* (Cambridge: Cambridge University Press, 2013), 25–27.

Girard bought up assets of the closed first Bank of the United States and with them set up a bank of his own. Rather ingeniously, he skirted a Pennsylvania statute requiring banking partnerships to get a state charter. He was the only owner—there were no partners. A bested Pennsylvania legislature had to acquiesce to the sole-proprietorship Bank of Stephen Girard, as it was by name. The Girard bank issued currency, payable on demand at the bank, and those banks that corresponded with it, in gold or silver. The notes, or currency, of this bank, denominated in dollars, remain for sale in the market for collectibles today.

The system worked in the following manner. A depositor would bring gold, silver, a corresponding bank's currency, or perhaps a government bond or another financial instrument to place in an account. The Girard bank would accept the deposit and give the depositor access to it according to a schedule (when the bank was open, on three occasions a month, etc.). The depositor making periodic withdrawals would generally take these in currency, currency issued by that bank and denominated in dollars.

Local banks, and in Girard's case those far afield, would accept this currency at face value, or sometimes at a "discount," as it was called, of perhaps 1 percent. The discount represented the cost of providing the acceptance service and an insurance premium on the chance that on redemption at the home institutions, there would be no gold or silver payable for the currency.

On giving the depositor the currency, the original deposit, typically made in gold or silver, remained in whole a holding of the bank's. The bank lent money on the basis of this capital, again in currency issued by the bank and redeemable at it and corresponding institutions in gold or silver at the dollar rate set by Congress. It is important to observe that outside of war emergencies, the only issuers of currency were the banks (including the Banks of the United States). Governments did not issue currency. As Daniel Webster explained it before the Supreme Court in 1839, what defines a bank is the "power to issue promissory notes with a view to their circulation as money." And as banking theorist Lysander Spooner noted in 1844, "the right of banking, or of contracting debts by giving promissory notes for the payment of money"—classically, gold or silver—"is as much a natural right, as that of manufacturing cotton."[26]

By principles such as these, banks issued currency to depositors making withdrawals and to clients taking loans to the degree that the bank's owners and managers felt that the currency would not quickly come back to them for redemption. If the executives felt that economic activity was acute or quickening, they would decide to issue notes to a greater degree; if they saw the reverse, they would become more conservative in their currency issuance. Their currency issuance could easily exceed the precious metals and other assets making up their capital. This capital could be a "fraction" (below one) of the currency outstanding—hence the term "fractional reserve banking."

In the operations of hundreds, and soon thousands, of banks across the economically maturing country, untold numbers of bankers had to make the call on issuing currency. They were "on the spot," in Hayek's phrase. And to recall Wanniski's observation on the feedback loop: "the bank always knows when it is printing one dollar too many, because it will show up

---

[26] Hammond, *Banks and Politics in America*, 690; *Collected Works of Lysander Spooner (1834–1886)*, vol. I 1834–1850 (Indianapolis: Liberty Fund, 2018), 186. Also see Spooner, *Two Treatises on Competitive Currency and Banking*, ed. Phillip W. Magness (American Institute of Economic Research, 2018).

somewhere in the economy and the person holding it will come to the bank and ask for gold. That little-bitty signal is all the [bank] needs to know at the end of the business day. If there is nobody at the gold window with surplus dollars and nobody at the dollar window with surplus gold, you know you are perfect in your management of the dollar."

Here is where the money supply gained its "elasticity." Gold and silver no longer sufficed for the total needs of the burgeoning economy because the production of these precious metals could not keep up with the general rate of economic growth. Therefore, a paper claim on gold or silver, created by innumerable dedicated observers, arose to supply good money. The supply was expandable because it was paper currency, plus credits extended to borrowers. And this supply was good because it permitted the portfolio preference to operate without inhibition. If people wanted to exchange their currency for precious metals, they could. This "feedback loop" was essential to the money supply's being just right.

Can it really have been just right? By modern reconstructions, the price stability record of this era was something modern central bankers can only aspire to. Throughout the 1830s, the consumer price index barely changed. In the years 1840 and 1860, prices of comparable goods were similar. In between, there was a 10 percent deflation that was then erased by a comparable inflation. In all, in the generation prior to the Civil War, prices changed perhaps 1 percent per year around a long-term par. Meanwhile, the scope and availability of goods and services were undergoing a profound transformation. There were so many new things every year that were affordable given one's current resources. In this era of prices close to steady at par, capital was freely available to finance the big opening stages of the Industrial Revolution. The money supply was indeed just right.

There was the odd financial panic, such as in 1819 and 1837. Government played a central role in each one. The 1819 affair reflected a banking system not able to muster the Herculean power needed to absorb the absurd amount of notes created under government auspices through 1815 during the War of 1812. If the tariff had been a little less severe, making real wages and the return rate on investment and the demand for capital a little higher, the difficulties might have been averted. A remark a Boston bank president made several decades later, in 1842, is telling on this score. An affiliated bank in Maine wanted to issue more currency, but the Boston executive warned, "with the new tariff and sub-treasury staring in our faces we think it unwise for banks to expand." Tariffs decreased return on investment, and the subtreasury (a plan to remove all federal funds from the banking system) promised to "sterilize" a large sum of gold and silver as unusable in the banking system. Assessing conditions "on the spot," the bank president advised curtailing the issuance of currency.[27]

As for 1837, during the three years prior the United States had pursued a massive sale of its own public lands, requiring on Jackson's "Specie Circular" order in 1836 exclusively gold or silver as payment. Prices were artificially low. The government widely accepted the minimum price of $1.25 per acre, even though a robust auction might get more. This distorted the allocation of capital in the economy, compelling investors to curtail current projects for the sweet deal of underpriced land.

---

[27] D.R. Whitney, *The Suffolk Bank* (Cambridge Mass: The Riverside Press, 1878), 38.

In turn came large withdrawals of precious metals from the banking system, lessening (artificially) the comparative demand for currency. Further government decisions included the federal government's playing favorites with which banks were getting its deposits, as well as states' taking out large loans, as federal land sales within state borders soared, in anticipation of windfalls of property tax revenue.

The second Bank of the United States did not get its charter renewed. Indeed, in 1833, it lost federal deposits and curtailed its lending. President Jackson prevailed in letting the charter of the bank lapse, largely on the strength of constitutional arguments that the federal government had no authority to launch, invest in, and participate in the directing of such an institution. After 1833, where the government would deposit its own money became a hot topic, leading to questions about which banks might benefit from gaining such liabilities. In brief, government policy exacerbated whatever economic crisis was brewing prior to 1837. Had the government auctioned off land like a normal private seller (as Henry George would urge after the Civil War) and accepted regular bank currency for it (like virtually everyone else did in economic transactions), as well as managed the transition of its own deposits into the extant banking network, it is reasonable to suppose that the Panic of 1837 would have been a minor event.

The second Bank of the United States folded at last, a private entity since 1836, in 1841. Owing to the barb of an editorial cartoon in the 1790s, the Bank of England, the crown's version of the Bank of the United States, was known colloquially as the "Old Lady of Threadneedle Street," after its location in London. This English crone was old in the 1790s yet has lived on even to this day. In contrast, the two Banks of the

United States were strictly confined to their age. They were each of them a Lady Antebellum, creatures that expired in the first half of the nineteenth century for a lack of want of or interest in what they had to offer.

The free-banking era

Today, the Federal Reserve, foreign central banks, and the International Monetary Fund—the major bureaucratic institutions directing the current monetary system—are the not properly ladylike institutions that the maturation of Bitcoin and cryptocurrency bid to make obsolete. The Federal Reserve, for example, issues currency, and the banking system it regulates issues credit. Bitcoin and crypto promise to take over these functions wholesale. Bitcoin, in its emulation of gold—limited in supply, clunky, aboriginal, aspiring to be a transferable store of value—stands to be final money. Ether, the lead follower, in its emulation of silver—limited but vaster in supply, easier to use commercially, a more preferred medium of active merchants—stands to be an example of alternative final money. Once the market capitalizations of Bitcoin and, say, Ether or Bitcoin offshoots grow to the point at which no power can take them over—if that outcome can be entertained—their prices may well stabilize. At that moment, there will be a Bitcoin/ major cryptocurrency alternatives ratio. Perhaps there will also be a stable Bitcoin/gold ratio. A definition of currency, of monetary credit, will have materialized, all without the services of the legacy bureaucratic institutions. Stablecoins could be issued on the basis of the ratio and be redeemable in fixed quantities of Bitcoin or the major alternatives or gold—like privately generated paper dollars used to be redeemable in gold or silver in the

1830s. Or stable-in-ratio Bitcoin and the alternatives and gold could be used in the marketplace—like gold and silver were in the 1830s.

The transition from the era of the second Bank of the United States to the "state" or "free" banking era, the period of the mid-1830s until 1861, is perhaps the one historical development most relevant to what Bitcoin and cryptocurrency promise to accomplish at the expense of our current monetary system. This roughly quarter-century was the time that absent any federal banking institutions, private issuance of currency sprouted up as never before or since.

In this period, there were some two thousand dollar-issuing banks, about half of them newly founded. After the demise of the second Bank of the United States, states liberalized their banking laws. Variously, these enabled banks either to operate under a state charter or simply to fulfill certain general require-ments to be permitted to operate. The latter were known as "free banks." The general requirements included such things as a certain reserve deposit of state or federal bonds and a restric-tion not to branch.

As the new banks, and the specie-redeemable dollar bills with their names on them, emerged, bankers and customers alike refined common practices for dealing with a growing mul-titude of currency issuers. Generally, if a bank received from a customer a dollar from another bank, that dollar was honored to the degree that the issuing bank was geographically close. This accounted for two things. The first was the cost of travel to the other bank. The issuing bank, and nowhere else, was the place where that bank's currency could be redeemed for gold or silver on demand. Therefore, if another bank accepted the currency, there would be a cost associated with any attempt at redemption. The second was the possibility that the issuing bank would not honor the redemption request. If this happened even one time, however, states would shut the offending bank down.

"Discounts" of dollars issued by banks across the country generally averaged about 2 percent. The discount was closer to nil for local banks and as high as 17 percent for Michigan banks, which were known for insolvency. State requirements for free banks to hold significant quantities of state bonds (making the banks not so free) increased the risk of insolvency. About 30 percent of free banks failed—meaning they could not keep every noteholder whole through the bank's close—with the biggest spike in failures coming in 1860–61 as the Civil War loomed. When a bank failed in such a fashion, note-holders got a share of the assets.[28]

On the crucial metric, the currency system of this era succeeded masterfully. Economic growth was stellar. On modern reckonings, economic output rose by some 4.5 percent per annum from the mid-1830s to 1860, an ample long-term figure. Meanwhile, prices of regular items stayed stable while all sorts of new products emerged. The big rise in incomes meant that everyone could buy and invest in what they used to and then some. The essential indicator of whether a monetary system works is how well the economy does under the auspices of that system. On this imperative standard, the free-banking era delivered.

Today, inflation takes away percentage points of currency values every year. In 2022, the rate was 8 percent per annum.

---

[28] Mathew Jaremski, "Bank-Specific Default Risk in the Pricing of Bank Note Discounts," *JEH* 71, no. 4 (Dec. 2011), 963; Jaremski, "Free Bank Failures: Risky Bonds versus Undiversified Portfolios," *Journal of Money, Credit and Banking* 42, no. 8 (Dec. 2010), 1570–71.

In April 1980, the rate was 18 percent. Regularly from the mid-1980s through 2020, the rate was 3 percent. Currency transaction costs across regions of the country today—lucky modern Americans—are nil. Privately issued dollars of the mid-nineteenth century cannot be said to have done worse than the Federal Reserve dollar in its day. And again, the record of economic growth during the free-banking era crushes that of the era of the Federal Reserve dollar.

Problems that might appear natural to the private issue of precious-metal-defined currency were, with dedication, overcome in this period. Customers, merchants, and bankers alike recognized counterfeiting and deliberate overprinting almost immediately. If currency issuers did such things, their reputations were shot. Therefore it was a minor problem. The Suffolk Bank of Boston was the leading entrepreneur in resolving these matters within the private sector. Suffolk required a deposit of some $5,000 from any distant bank that wished to have its currency accepted there. "Country" banks squealed at the requirement, but they paid in. In a recollection by one of the Suffolk bankers of these times, the banker noted that "constant warnings…run all through the correspondence of the bank. Neither was the bank willing to enter into any correspondence with any new banks for the redemption of their bills, thus giving them credit, unless it was satisfied that the public would be safe in taking them." Are bank fraud detection measures so stellar now?[29]

Accusations that the banks of this period—in particular, "wildcats" seeking to pass bad currency—were a pox upon the economy have proven unfounded. A Federal Reserve study of

---

[29]   Whitney, *The Suffolk Bank*, 38.

1996 found that in the practices of the leading free-banking state of New York, after a rough start in the early 1840s, note clearance among free banks improved such that only 0.1 percent of notes and deposits were not cleared at par in the 1850s. Among the states with larger below-par closure rates, the culprit was not an overproduction of currency—but rather large declines in the capital asset, namely state bonds. Ratings publications, first developed for commercial agents by abolitionist Lewis Tappan in the 1840s, made it clearer which currency issuers were reputable, as well as provided incentives for currency issuers to be reputable. The period of 1833–60 vindicated the initial wisdom of the take-off of the Industrial Revolution. Gold and silver are final money, and the financing of business ventures through private currency defined in those precious metals is a route to steady prices, the respect of portfolio preferences, information feedback loops, fantastic economic growth, and the emergence of mass prosperity.[30]

Historian Robert Sylla emphasized that after 1790, "U.S. economic growth was 'finance-led.'" He found that "the developing American economy generated a demand for money that grew even faster than it did in the colonial era, and banks met the demand. The main effect of the banking innovation was to supply at relatively modest expense an unprecedented demand for money that was far beyond the capacity of existing stocks of gold and silver to meet." As Sylla's collaborator Robert E. Wright put it, "intermediaries were able to funnel the savings of many investors, large and small, to wealth-producing business

---

[30] Gerald P. Dwyer, "Wildcat Banking, Banking Panics, and Free Banking in the United States," Federal Reserve Bank of Atlanta *Economic Review* 81, no. 3 (Dec. 1996), 9. See also the work of George Selgin on state banking in the nineteenth century, e.g., "The Fable of the Cats," ALT-M *Cato at Liberty*, July 2, 2021, at www.cato.org/blog/fable-cats.

firms, including manufacturers. The development of financial intermediaries…preceded, and to some extent even directed, general economic development." As banks collected savings, they developed a "monetary base" that they used for redemption requests, while they issued money, dollars, in excess of that base to the degree that business acumen dictated. The results were stupendous. Among innumerable examples was Lackawanna Iron and Coal. As it strove to make rail factories from scratch in eastern Pennsylvania in the 1840s, the founders staked their mortgages for bank loans. The loans represented bets on the success of the enterprise—which came in fantastic dimensions, eventually, for this company (it became the largest steel company in the country prior to the founding of United States Steel in 1901). That very success justified the new dollars called into creation at the firm's beginning.[31]

What instability there was in the free banking era came from governmental meddling. Free banks often had to have state bonds as their reserves. State governments used the free banks as compulsory customers. Free banks failed more than charter banks (which had less restrictive reserve requirements) because state bonds were a risky asset (state defaults were legion in the aftermath of the Panic of 1837). States also did not permit banks to branch. Risk was more difficult to disperse and therefore mitigate, and currency discounts increased because

---

[31] Richard Sylla, "U.S. Securities Markets and the Banking System, 1790–1840," Federal Reserve Bank of St. Louis *Review* 80, no. 3 (May/June 1998), 97; Sylla, "Monetary Innovation in America," 26; Robert E. Wright, review of "A History of Banking in Antebellum America," *Journal of Interdisciplinary History* 32, no. 1 (Summer 2001), 140; W. David Lewis, "The Early History of the Pennsylvania Iron and Coal Company: A Study in Technological Adaptation," *Pennsylvania Magazine of History and Biography* 96, no. 4 (Oct. 1972), 436–439.

of the distances between banks across the states. In Scotland and Canada, banks branched and had smaller failure rates than in the United States. In 1857, Congress reduced the monetary base by declaring foreign coin no longer legal dollars. If people (including bank managers) wanted to use foreign coin as dollars, they had to take the lot to the Mint to be melted and struck as United States coins (the profits going to the government). Despite these inhibitions, in the several decades before the Civil War, when Americans were largely left alone to set up dollar-creating enterprises, freedom in banking and currency issuance worked—and the economy boomed.

Toward a Federal Takeover

The first casualty of war is truth, to paraphrase Samuel Johnson. The financial truth casualty of the Civil War remains apprehensible today. The Department of the Treasury's Office of the Comptroller of the Currency posits the following on its website:

> President Lincoln recognized that unreliable paper money and inadequate credit was problematic....
>
> Through the National Bank Act [of 1864 and an allied act of the previous year], Congress sought to achieve both short- and long-term goals. One crucial objective was to generate cash desperately needed to finance and fight the Civil War....Prospective national bank organizers...were required to purchase interest-bearing U.S. government bonds.... Millions of

much-needed dollars flowed into the Treasury in this manner.

But the national banking system was also designed to achieve longer term economic goals. Under the new system, the purchased [exclusively federal] bonds were to be deposited with the Treasury, where they were held as security for a new kind of paper money: national currency. Bearing the name of the issuing national bank and the signatures of its officers, these notes were otherwise identical in design, size, and coloration. Anyone holding a national bank note could present it for redemption, in gold or silver coin, at the issuing bank or at reserve banks around the country. If, for whatever reason, the issuing bank was unable to meet the demand for cash redemption, the system was set up so that the government could sell the bank's bonds and pay off the noteholders directly.

Once accepting and holding national currency became essentially risk-free, it gained in public confidence and circulated throughout the nation. This represented a marked improvement over the pre-Civil War money supply, which had involved thousands of different varieties of paper money issued by local banks, rampant counterfeiting, chronic uncertainty about the value of paper money, and, as a result, difficulty conducting private business.

> Through the more orderly national money and banking system, Congress sought to promote economic growth and prosperity and a stronger sense of American nationalism.

To stress the point again, on modern reconstructions, the real economic growth rate of the United States in the generation immediately preceding the Civil War, from 1830 to 1860, was 4.5 percent per year, while prices slightly varied around a par. Economic growth such that the economy doubled in size every sixteen years as prices stayed the same—this was the era, per the Treasury Comptroller's rendering in the 2020s, in which "chronic uncertainty about the value of paper money" resulted in "difficulty conducting private business." Travel freight up five hundred times in the forty years to 1855, the whale-oil bonanza soon to be rendered moot with the Pennsylvania petroleum discoveries of 1859 (which would catch John D. Rockefeller's eye), the bumper crops cleared at market, all must be cast aside to sustain the contention that "difficulty conducting private business" prevailed in the private-currency, free-banking era before 1861.[32]

Financial historian Timberlake saw things differently:

> The banking and monetary system on the eve of the Civil War had enjoyed fifteen years of relative stability, a condition often aspired to by secretaries of the Treasury during that era. Strangely enough, historians and analysts have

---

[32] "Founding of the OCC & the National Banking System," Office of the Comptroller of the Currency, at www.occ.treas.gov/about/who-we-are/history/founding-occ-national-bank-system/index-founding-occ-national-banking-system.html.

not given the era a good press. [One prominent historian], for example, saw the currency system as "far from satisfactory." There was, he said, "no central place of redemption, hence most notes were at a discount, varying with the distance from the bank of issue. It was estimated that there were 7000 kinds and denominations of notes, and fully 4000 spurious or altered varieties were reported."

The appearance of wildcat banks [banks that sprung up with little apparent regulation] supposedly was symptomatic of these "chaotic" banking conditions. Yet neither [this historian] nor other historians have offered much hard evidence to support such a dismal picture. In fact, a recent study…reliably indicates that by 1860 note holders' losses from all "free" banks, including wildcats, were less than they would have lost in that year from a 2 percent inflation.

In the present day, banks and regulatory agencies assess their depositors user fees that are comparable, if they do not exceed, the losses from bad currency in the free-banking era. Small-balance charges, minimum balances, low rates of interest, taxes for deposit insurance, and banking regulation, along with a secular inflation easily exceeding 2 percent in contemporary America ensure a high price for holding money at a modern bank. A minimum of 2 percent yearly inflation, it might be added, is the standard central bank aspirational policy goal of our age. Under the 8 percent inflation of 2022, an average worker who takes two or three weeks off loses another four weeks' worth of pay from inflation.[33]

As Timberlake summarized his view, "the records for the period 1845–1860 imply an economic tranquility that contradicts this critical view of…the monetary system." But "the Civil War put an end to these idyllic conditions. Its real demands on the economies of both North and South were long-run and pervasive, as were its institutional effects on the banking and monetary systems."[34]

Not letting a crisis go to waste

War remakes the home front—an adage of history. The private issuance of currency, based on precious metals, got the shock of its life with the Civil War monetary and banking acts of Congress. The changes were permanent. They solidified into their own mold with the creation of the Federal Reserve in 1913. The financial needs of the federal, the Union, government during the war were enormous. The United States spent about $3 billion from 1861 to 1865, five times as much as in the decade of the 1850s. A hiked-up tariff set in place in 1861 and a questionably constitutional new income tax of 1862 were not enough to reel in the revenue. The federal debt increased by fortyfold, or by $2.5 billion, from 1860 to 1865.

The Civil War tax measures decreased the return rate on investments. This had profound consequences for the currency system. Companies had to pay their workers more for the same work to make up for the increase in prices that came with the tariff. Profit margins went down. When the reduced profits then

---

[33] Timberlake, *Monetary Policy in the United States*, 84.
[34] Timberlake, *Monetary Policy in the United States*, 84–85.

came to affluent investors (those mainly liable for the income tax), upwards of 10 percent had to go to that tax. Each dollar of investment saw its rate of return go down owing to the wartime political-economic measures. Therefore, the demand for loan funds—loans made in currency—went down. The demand for currency's redemption asset, specie, went up.

The private-issue currency system that had been flourishing in recent years had emerged organically to finance, at a profit, an economy at peace interested in discovering new vistas of its productive potential. It was not appropriate for wartime conditions. The comprehensiveness of the war, coupled with the new war taxes, guaranteed that demand for money for non-war-related investments was falling to nil. Furthermore, banks would be loath to issue redeemable money to the government or its contractors, given that these entities were not the forces of economic growth. The situation came to a head in December 1861. New York and Philadelphia banks, with regional banks following their lead, announced that they would no longer redeem notes for gold or silver. Congress did the same, suspending specie payments for federal debt instruments. This situation held for the next seventeen years, until New Year's 1879.

After the December 1861 suspension, the United States was free to take emergency currency measures. The first, of February 1862, was to declare that federally created paper currency—which the government had not issued on any scale since the 1812 war (paper currency in the intervening five decades being almost exclusively the creation of banks)—was "legal tender." If you offered something for sale in the United States, you had to take this federal currency, "greenbacks," as they were known for their color. They were not redeemable in gold or anything else (just like Britain's pound in the Napoleonic era).

The assumption was that the Union would win the war, peace would be restored, taxes would go down, investment demand would boom, this currency would be useful, and in time, what remained in circulation after the government retired some of it collected in tax receipts could be redeemed in precious metals.

The market price of gold and silver went up sharply against the legal tender greenbacks. Gold about doubled, hitting over forty dollars per ounce in 1864 in private New York transactions. An ounce of silver, the definition of the dollar, almost tripled to nearly three dollars. Consumer price inflation in the legal tender, non-specie-defined greenback currency took hold. It totaled about 100 percent from 1861 to 1865. Merchants took the greenbacks as the law said they must, but only after doubling their prices. Money held as savings in dollars went down by half. The Treasury issued greenbacks through the end of the war in 1865.

The second change was the long-lasting one. It is that referred to in the recounting of the origins of the "national banking system" on the Treasury website quoted above. In a series of pieces of legislation from 1862 to 1864, Congress encouraged banks, once again, to produce their own currency. There would be a new countrywide system for this purpose. Congress would name certain banks throughout the country as "national banks" and authorize them to issue "national" currency. Each bank was required to have a reserve in federal government bonds that would be the basis of its currency issuance (in the twentieth century, thanks to moves by President Franklin Roosevelt, mortgages would also serve in this role). In the past, precious metals and, in certain instances, state bonds had this function. That was done away with. Congress taxed all currency not issued under its new system, killing off such currency. As for reserves in gold or silver, banks had no interest in redeeming at the official price, about twenty dollars per ounce of gold and one dollar for silver. Gold and silver were fetching upwards of double or triple these prices in the markets as Congress mandated the national banking system. The Mint, for its part, rejiggered the making of the half-dime. Having always been silver, it was now a "nickel" made out of that cheaper material because the silver making up half-dimes cost more than five cents.

Beginning in 1863 and lasting for decades, "national bank notes" came out of the favored "national banks," so named by the federal authorities, across the country. These were predominantly the "US dollars" of this period. They ranged in denominations up from one dollar. This development represented an arrogation on the part of the federal power away from the diverse, private, organic banking status quo of the prewar period. It was the first step toward eliminating those pillars of currency production that had been identified by Daniel Webster and Lysander Spooner in the productive years of the period between the second Bank of the United States and the Civil War. For Webster, the very definition of a bank was that institution that freely acted to make currency. For Spooner, making money for sale as one saw fit was as natural a business impulse as manufacturing an ordinary staple such as cotton.

As the war ended in 1865, Congress became concerned about what might happen to the greenbacks. Legal tender conceivably required a police state, forcing people to take such non-specie-defined currency. What if people preferred not to take it? Accepting greenbacks in war, when the appeals to patriotism have traction, is one thing. It is quite another in the normal comings-and-goings of peace. Congress decided on a two-pronged strategy. First, at war's end it would seek to retire the greenbacks as much as possible. It would accept them as payment of taxes and then destroy a portion. Of the some $450 million in greenbacks outstanding in 1864, about $70 million had been collected and retired by the government within five years.

Greenbacks, a congressionally guided national banking system, a hiked-up tariff, and a modest income tax—the major political-economic measures of the Civil War—all remained in the peace that came after 1865. It is important to note that the United States economy performed with the utmost splendidness in the decades after the Civil War. The rates of economic growth, as they are calculated today, remain the best in history. The two greatest decades of economic growth (excluding the growth of government) across the American experience are the 1870s and the 1880s. Growth totaled 70 percent in the 1870s and another 68 percent in the 1880s. This is when housing first became roomy, modern, available, and networked into heating, water, and other systems; food production, transport, and storage enabled urbanization and cosmopolitan culture; and best business practices (typified by Rockefeller's Standard Oil, founded in 1870) emphasized excellent new products and service to the utmost satisfaction of the customer. The list of new products and services, and improvements to old ones, is of necessity impossible to enumerate. This was the exponential curve inclusive of its massive integral underneath—the huge expansion in economic production that left precedent in the dust.

Therefore the national banking system worked? It is not so simple as that. Several developments early in the national banking era were surely essential to its unfolding success. The first was the rapid retirement of the Civil War debt. The National

Banking Acts of the Civil War years perhaps implied that the government would keep debt highly available for national bank reserves. This did not happen. After 1866, Congress and the Treasury focused on debt retirement to a degree unheard of in modern times. After retiring greenbacks for a few years, Congress quit that in place of paying off the federal debt, which had peaked at $2.8 billion in 1866. From the late 1860s to the early 1890s, the debt went down remorselessly. In 1893, it totaled $1.5 billion. In a quarter-century, the debt was taken down by 45 percent, as the economy more than tripled in size. To do the same in 2023, the United States would have had to reduce its debt by $15 trillion. Indeed, if it had done this, the private economy just might have been poised to triple in size afterward.

In the classic interpretation by historian Jeffrey G. Williamson of 1974, the rapid retirement of the Civil War debt greatly enhanced the diversity of the productive resources of the American investor class. As the government bought up its own bonds held by monied Americans, these rich people had more to devote to other kinds of assets—assets in the private sector that, with further bolstering and attention, could become very productive. As Williamson put it, "government debt retirement should foster a comparable expansion in private debt"—which is to say, in private titles to ownership of enterprise assets—"and thus in measured private capital formation." He added, "individual savers may be indifferent between public and private debt in satisfying wealth accumulation motives, providing, of course, that Treasury officials offer government debt at rates competitive with more risky private debt, but the presence of government debt clearly implies lower levels of private capital stock and lower levels of future GNP."[35]

The second policy that contributed to growth after 1865 was that the United States dismantled a part of its tax system. It retained the tariff and put on sales taxes (chiefly on alcohol), but it did away with the income tax experiment. Total government spending fell rapidly after 1865 and stayed at a low level. By 1888, federal spending was down to 2.3 percent of GDP, merely decimal places higher than the pre-1860 norm. State and local spending stood at about 3.5 percent of GDP, up a percentage point from before the war. These increases were the beginning of a "ratchet effect," as described by Robert Higgs drawing upon James Madison, whereby after a crisis, a government declines to shrink to the level it had occupied before. The ratchet effect was small for years after the Civil War. Government spending was 5.8 percent of economic output—today, it is distinctive when the percentage in the United States is under 35. France's ratio as of 2019 stood at 55.[36]

There was little bar to investments in this environment. One obstacle was that wages paid by business owners had to be higher because of the protective tariff; otherwise labor would hold out against a nominal wage lessened in real value by the tariff. (Lower tariff rates, as Congress discussed throughout the nineteenth century, would have brought in more customs revenue, per the Laffer curve.) And wages paid had to be higher

---

[35] Jeffrey G. Williamson, "Watersheds and Turning Points: Conjectures on the Long-Term Impact of Civil War Financing," *JEH* 34, no. 3 (Sept. 1974), 644–45.

[36] Readers of Higgs named the "ratchet effect" as such. Higgs used the term "ratchet" repeatedly in his foundational work, Robert Higgs, *Crisis and Leviathan: Critical Episodes in the Growth of American Government* (New York: Oxford University Press), 1987.

because of taxes on alcohol and various consumer sundries. But that was it. No income taxes, no levies on capital gains, no corporate taxes. What one made in investments, in a business after expenses, one kept. The participant belonged in the economy. If one succeeded at work, the material profit accrued to the participant in full. It was a stimulus to participate, to grow the society.

When the government relieved, at market prices, so many holders of their government debt, they were (per the Williamson effect) quick to devote their investable cash to productive private investments. The barrier to the productivity of these investments (aside from the protective elements of the tariff) was the financing of government at all of 5.8 percent of GDP. Indeed, as Williamson notes, foreigners started buying up the Civil War debt in subsequent years, even as the federal government was trying to retire it, because their home environment was not as good as America's for private investment. Americans were raising cash all over the place in the years after 1865 to plow it into the varied and immense economic projects that characterized the great boom that made their economy, in that period, the largest in the world and quite arguably the greatest in history.

Surely, a major reason the national banking system succeeded is that the political-economic system, particularly regarding taxes and spending, took on restraint. Had there been comprehensive taxation and high tax rates after 1865, or large sustained increases in government outlays, it is fanciful to imagine that there would have been demand for money anywhere near the level recorded. A paradox of the national banking system is that it required dollar-issuers to hold federal debt as their reserve asset. It was paradoxical because the United States was busy retiring that debt. Yet this paradox is probably the secret to the whole question. The national banking system, whatever the pronouncements of Congress and the Treasury, had the aspect of a temporary program. The government, inclusive of its debt instruments, was set on diminishing itself. On current trends, there was no compelling reason to believe that government bonds would be the basis for private currency issuance for much longer. Surely something suggestive of the *status quo ante* was waiting in the wings to take up the traditional role of monetary base money. And there was—gold.

The era of the gold standard

In the heat of the national crisis of 1861–65, the national banking system made do with the circumstances. The official redemption price of gold and silver felt market pressure in 1861 and had to be abandoned. The price of specie soared in the markets thereafter. The idea that private banks would issue currency in the congressionally defined dollar price, of some twenty dollars for an ounce of gold and one dollar for silver, became moot. The arbitrage opportunity would have been ridiculous. Get paid in a twenty-dollar note, take it to the bank for the ounce of gold, and then get forty dollars on the market for that ounce of gold. The market price of precious metals was high because of the war, because of its destruction and how it limited the potential for real investment, let alone the greenback issue. The shuttering of private or state-bank currency had nothing to do with any inherent "instability" in the received system. The emergence of a national bank system was a function of the war.

Like the tariff of 1861—but unlike the income tax and the greenbacks—the national bank system stayed after 1865, for more than half a century. In 1913, both the tariff and the national bank system would largely, but not completely, meet their demise, the former through the new income tax, the latter through the Federal Reserve. The tariff had been in existence since 1789. Increasing it in 1861 was part of a long history of that tax regime's waxing and waning. The national bank system was a financial reform first made in wartime and sustained in peace. Not in the various foreign hostilities of the Federal period, not in the War of 1812, and not in the Mexican War had financial policy changes in view of war exigencies settled in as a permanent new system for peacetime. In this, the national bank system was unique.

Any argument that the national banking system brought order to typical American monetary chaos is therefore a strained one. During the war, the United States badly needed people to buy its bonds. Mandating these bonds as bank reserves was one way of encouraging this result. The cheerleading for the national banking system of the latter-day Treasury indulges in circular logic: federal bonds had to be bought during the Civil War; therefore, when they were bought, largely because they had to be by the new national banks, the previous way of doing things in banking and currency issuance was flawed. A simpler way of putting it is that the war wiped out the possibility of specie redemption, the federal government taxed away the state and free-banking systems, and then it used its huge new issue of bonds as the pretext for the national bank system.

Another option was, perhaps, for Congress to have devalued the dollar. Perhaps Congress could have made the dollar officially redeemable at forty dollars per ounce in gold and two dollars in silver. This was not a palatable option. Such a course of action probably would have led to an abandonment of the dollar abroad. The word in foreign locales would have been that the Americans have a currency that on their sudden legislative diktat, occasioned by a domestic disturbance, loses half its value. One day, twenty dollars is worth five British pounds, and the next day, two-and-a-half. Moreover, there was variation in the precious metal dollar prices in this period of American upheaval. Gold went up in steps in the markets to over forty dollars as the greenbacks came in, and silver followed a similar course. The market price of precious metals has to be near the mint or "strike" (as in striking a coin with a denomination on it) price for the system to work. This is accomplished by ensuring a robust demand for coin and currency via an outstanding business environment.

Therefore, the United States also opted for a third kind of national currency in the Civil War. Aside from the federally issued greenbacks, the national bank notes with the backing of US bonds, the Treasury also offered "gold certificates." These were dollar notes (denominations beginning at twenty dollars) redeemable by the Treasury at the original gold price of $20.67 per ounce. The purpose of these notes was to maintain the flow of federal financing. The government did not permit customs duties to be paid in greenbacks or even national bank notes. These had to come in gold or gold certificates. Likewise, the federal government did not pay interest on its debt (largely held by foreigners) in greenbacks or their like in national bank notes, because demand for that debt would dry up. These payments came in gold or gold certificates.

It is a common practice for countries engaged in war or war planning to have a two-tier currency system: the fiat currency for domestic purposes and the hard currency for external and government-financing purposes. National Socialist Germany in the 1930s had such a setup, as did the Soviet Union throughout its history. In the United States after 1865 (when the Treasury first managed to get gold certificates printed), these dollars were usable for domestic transactions. But they traded at a premium to greenbacks and national bank notes.

It is understandable that governments might look upon Bitcoin and cryptocurrency with trepidation. Government dominance of the currency system appears to be essential to the prosecution of those quintessential governmental functions, warfare and the quelling of domestic disturbances. Nonetheless, a private currency system can provide a basis for domestic economic transactions, even in the circumstances of war and disturbance, perhaps superior to that of a government. The efficiency loss that came to the economy with the upending of the price system in the Civil War, for example, perhaps would have been not so severe if private currencies were left to flourish. And private economic efficiency is the foundation of the government fisc.

Reserving banking for the best people

The strain of attitude in American political culture opposed to fully private banking and currency issuance, alive throughout the nineteenth century, played a role in the creation of the national banking system. The advocates and heirs of the first and second Banks of the United States finally got another way, in the Civil War, to assert federal primacy in the making of money. In the antebellum period, these people had coalesced within the Whig political party. The Whigs reconstituted themselves in the 1850s, incorporating with other political elements into the Republican party. The old Whig Abraham Lincoln's Republicans had operational majorities throughout the government during the war.

Whigs had characteristically felt that there was a sort of natural class structure in the United States, that certain individuals know what they are doing and have self-control more than others. These individuals generally should be the ones in charge. Not to set up prerogative-filled federal institutions such as the Bank of the United States where such individuals could find their range to operate would be to fail to admit that there is such a thing as the best people. The surpassing historian of the Whigs, Daniel Walker Howe, found that the Whigs felt this way about their own internal psychology. Each person has various impulses, and the better should subordinate the worse. As Howe wrote:

> Within [Whig] faculty psychology, the highest value was balance, that is, the proper expression of each human power but the excessive indulgence of none. The idea was not easily implemented.... [B]alance could be attained only by careful self-control. Unfortunately, the strength of the faculties varied inversely with their position in the sequence of rightful precedence. Left to themselves, the lower powers would escape control and wreak havoc.... The good life entailed continual self-discipline....

> Like countless others before them, the American Whigs drew "the analogy between the human system and the social and political system"; Webster would liken the circulation of blood in an organism to the circulation of money in the marketplace. An essential feature of the analogy for the Whigs was the parallel between

> regulating the faculties within an individual
> and regulating the individuals within society....
> The model ruled out laissez-faire as a social
> philosophy, emphasizing instead the mutual
> responsibility of individuals and classes.

Whigs like Webster respected that banks created money but strongly preferred that those who ran the banks be persons of Whiggish probity. Perhaps a system with feedback loops—currency and monetary issues redeemable in a base entity as in classical monetary systems—naturally breeds a higher degree of probity among those who create and trade in the realms of economic life.[37]

Money in its circulation was a private, organic affair in the Whig view. But not at its point of origin. That should be the province of the best people. Such people are not incompetent, not fools, not speculators off to make a quick or dishonest buck, and not wildcatters. They are accomplished, public-spirited, prudent, educated, far-seeing, and willing to assert that they should be paid commensurately for their services. Not that any of this worked out to perfection in any given example. Stephen Girard, who was possibly the richest person in the country at the time and conspicuously public-minded, and thus a natural Whig paragon, quit the second Bank of the United States after a few years, citing its imperiousness.

The national banking system reflected the Whig model of society. The best banks from across the country would be permitted to issue US dollars on federal-bond security. A great number of existing banks, over one thousand, signed up to be

---

[37] Daniel Walker Howe, *The Political Culture of the American Whigs* (Chicago: University of Chicago Press, 1979), 29.

national banks and hoped for approval. Those who failed to get approval, or did not seek it, would be taxed (Marshall's "power to destroy") at least 10 percent per note if they tried to issue currency. It was very Whig. The quality people who cooperated with the federal system produced the money. Customers (drawn from society's rank-and-file for the most part) could choose to use that money as they saw fit in their humble, when not ill-starred, ways. Given a deference to government and hierarchy, the system would work out for the best.

One quality person as the national banking system settled in was the father of the future richest person in America, Andrew W. Mellon. When "Andy" was a boy of fourteen, in 1870, his father, Judge Thomas Mellon, set aside his career on the bench and founded a bank in Pittsburgh. Reflecting on the environment he stepped into, Thomas Mellon wrote, in his 1885 autobiography:

> At an early age I had seen the disasters produced by the great collapse of 1819, which followed the war of 1812; and expected a similar collapse after the late war, but had forgotten the fact that the collapse of 1819 was delayed so long after the war of 1812; and, in the present instance, the time of prosperity was so remarkably prolonged that I began to doubt my apprehensions, and to think it possible that some special virtue in our new greenback currency and national banking system had averted a collapse altogether. For a couple of years or so after the end of the Rebellion I had expected such a collapse and was fully prepared for it, and lost some fine opportunities by over

> cautiousness; but instead of a collapse business went on increasing and prices advancing. Such an excellent and reliable financial and banking system had never before existed in the country, and we were led to attribute the apparent prosperity and continued stability of affairs to it. This threw us off our guard, and… we allowed a large proportion of our own bank capital and deposits of both banks to be invested in mortgages and similar securities.

Thomas Mellon almost closed his bank's doors in a wipe-out in October 1873. He saved it by shortening his hours and asking depositors who did not really need their money to hold out on withdrawals. One example was an older Irish woman whose laborer husband had put away $1,600 over a lifetime of work. Had the Panic of 1873 claimed the nascent Mellon fortune, it is a fair question whether Gulf Oil, Alcoa, and other major enterprises that Andy and his brothers would coax into existence in the upcoming years, and that would change the world (aluminum in airplanes, for example), would have ever had a shot. The gross financial panic under the auspices of the national banking system in the early 1870s almost cost the twentieth century some of its most essential innovations.[38]

Stellar growth characterized the American economy in the late 1860s, the 1870s, and the 1880s, to be sure. But there was also a financial bubble and pop as the long opening act of the national banking system. Not of the free-banking system but of its rescuer and improvement, the national banking system.

---

[38] Thomas Mellon, *Thomas Mellon and His Times* (Pittsburgh: University of Pittsburgh Press, 1994), 245.

This was the one in which the chosen official currency-issuers based their money on United States Treasury bonds, not precious metals, and guaranteed each other's issues, as the Treasury itself did.

Again, the Comptroller of the Currency (an office created by the National Currency Act of 1863) in 2020: "Once accepting and holding national currency became essentially risk-free, it gained in public confidence and circulated throughout the nation. This represented a marked improvement over the pre-Civil War money supply…. Through the more orderly national money and banking system, Congress sought to promote economic growth and prosperity and a stronger sense of American nationalism."

What the risk-free national banking system superintended, if not promoted, in its immediate peacetime years was a run of popular speculation. Judge Mellon on the years before 1873:

> A mania existed in all classes for dealing in lots and other real estate, not alone for actual use but speculation. Every workingman and mechanic who had saved up any money invested in a lot, even if they could pay but a small portion of the purchase money, securing the balance on deferred payments. Even professional men and merchants joined the throng of purchasers. Our business in that line was conducted by private sales to individual applicants. But public sales was the general custom with others, who advertised extensively, and by means of brass bands and excursion trains, and the distribution of refreshments, would gather a crowd on the premises from time to time and

dispose of large numbers of lots at auction. At the same time that this excitement in lots and real estate sales was raging, new railroads were under course of construction in all directions, and railroad bonds, and stocks bearing high rates of interest were pressing for purchasers at temptingly low prices. Such was the condition of affairs when I left the bench, and until the general collapse of 1873.

Brass bands, refreshments, excursion trains—welcome workingman, welcome professional, here is a deal on acreage that can be divided into twelfths for housing. And they bought, on credit. Of course the national banks lent out. They guaranteed each other, the Treasury guaranteed them, and the notes they wrote could not come back to them with a demand for redemption in metal (that would only come after the lessons of experience in 1879). It was, oddly enough, an inversion of Whig priorities. The national banking system, in its initial phases, indulged and enabled the get-rich-quick element latent in common society and which many in business strive for. The better people were sidelined. Judge Mellon had "lost some fine opportunities by over cautiousness."[39]

By the fall of 1873, with total Treasury bonds outstanding (and thus potential bank reserves) down by a fifth in nominal, and considerably more in real terms, from the Civil War-era high, banks got skittish about issuing more notes and credit. It would become a trademark of the national banking system until the creation of the Federal Reserve. National banks, perhaps scared of being dropped from the system, shifted toward

---

[39] Mellon, *Thomas Mellon and His Times*, 246.

conservatism in their currency issuance. Their feedback loop prioritized staying in the system above all else. It was difficult for other currency issuers to step in, in that their currencies faced taxation for not being federally sanctioned national currency.

The Panic of 1873, and the depression that lasted through 1875, remains one of the most bitter of American history. To be sure, its reputation is exaggerated. The 1870s were the decade of the "Long Depression," with conditions persisting for perhaps even five-and-a-half years, according to the National Bureau of Economic Research. How this squares with the 1870s being the greatest of growth decades, of GDP expansion of 70 percent, is a question that has attracted renegade interest from economic historians such as Christina Romer. What is certain is that there were widespread examples of people being thrown out of work, persistence in unemployment (a word not coined until the 1890s), and assets lingering at sale prices. In the Great Railroad Strike of 1877, at least one hundred people were killed nationally in actions pitting pre-trade-union strikers against state militias, federal troops, the national guard, and private security forces. Large amounts of property caught fire or were otherwise destroyed. In Mellon's Pittsburgh, worker protesters set significant parts of the city aflame.

An occasion of that strike was a series of nominal pay reductions. These coincided—usually after a lag—with the deflation that had been chronic since the war's end in 1865. Consumer prices fell by about a third from 1865 to 1875. They then lost about another tenth from 1875 to 1879. One can argue that the strikers should have realized that their wages were sticky high before the reductions—a point that, in general terms, would fascinate economist John Maynard Keynes in the next century. One of the reasons for the deflation of the 1870s was that it was clear that the United States had to resume its monetary standard, its dollar at one dollar per circa an ounce of silver or twenty dollars for gold or both. The Treasury bond basis for currency had proven its weaknesses. People were willing to take out loans in this currency too much, on the understanding that the Treasury would guarantee the bond-based dollar irrespective of precious metals. Perhaps the Treasury would even countenance a devaluation or inflation. Banks had a similar sense of security regarding their currency issuance, at least until the panic. A final weakness was that it was clear that foreigners would not keep taking American paper currency, even if gold certificates were trading at a premium to greenbacks, unless their own was made whole against the entire lot of American money.

A particular fate became inescapable. There had to be a "resumption," as it was called, of a restoration of the circa twenty-dollar official gold price, if not the old official silver price as well. If it did not become increasingly clear that this was going to happen, the dollar after 1873 would be in jeopardy at home and abroad.

Therefore, Congress, prodded by the panic, took a series of steps indicating that by 1879, the United States would restore convertibility of the dollar in gold at the prewar price. This happened in January 1879. The Treasury opened its window to dollar redemptions in gold at the old price, at that time, to almost no takers. The national banks had to oblige as well, and they too saw little business. The promise floating around the economy since 1865 had been credible. The United States had wound down so much of its governmental expansion of the Civil War era that the profitability of private business was too great to go calling for gold when convertibility resumed in

1879. On Wanniski's rule, no one at the gold window means a banker can issue more currency.

The United States put the dollar back on gold at $20.67 per about an ounce in 1879. This added to the basis of the national banking system. Now, not only was currency issued on account of the Treasury bonds held by a national bank, but dollars were also redeemable at all national banks and the Treasury in gold. In a portentous development, silver was not included in the arrangement. Before, banks had redeemed currency not just in gold but in "specie," in gold or silver, at the rate given by Congress per the Constitution's clause on "regulate the Value thereof" pertaining to US-coined money. This ratio was sixteen silver to one gold after 1834.

For reasons that remain difficult to identify with confidence, after the war Congress began to prioritize gold over silver, Gresham's law in reverse perhaps. One concern was that new silver discoveries would prove too great and break the gold-silver ratio. Another was that rising countries like Germany were only on gold, as Britain had been for some time. Still another was, surely, that the United States had lost credibility internationally with the Civil War. "Now we are engaged in a great civil war, testing whether that nation, or any nation so conceived and so dedicated [as the United States], can long endure," as Lincoln said at Gettysburg. If the United States felt it needed to convince the world of its viability in 1865, it might have wished to guarantee its currency exclusively in the quintessential precious metal, gold. In the mid-1870s, the United States accepted silver for redemption in dollars but put caps on the total amount of silver the Treasury would take in.

As Timberlake wrote in 2013 about bimetallism, or the use of both gold and silver as an official monetary unit:

> [Bimetallism] had the advantage of not relying on one substance to provide a base medium for nominal growth of money to finance the economy's real productivity. If one metal became scarce, the other metal would take up the slack so that the common money stock could increase with the growth in real output.

And he warned, pertinent to the developments of the 1870s:

> Under a monometallic gold standard, the subsidiary silver coins, which were also legal tender, became similar to legal tender paper money. They were redeemable in gold coin…. However, it was just as much a fiat money…as a scruffy paper dollar dropped soundlessly on the counter for a similar purpose.

From the Coinage Act of 1792 until 1861, the War of 1812 years excepted, the thing that people could require as they redeemed their dollar currency was that they get either one of the twosome set of precious metals, gold or silver. Now, a means was introduced by which people could bring silver and demand gold. This had not been the case in the previous era. Silver had been final money just as much as gold.[40]

After 1879, the national banks were, with the federal government, the only entity that could issue untaxed dollars redeemable in gold. (The federal government continued to issue greenbacks, now called United States Notes, and redeemable in gold, but kept the total supply outstanding static.) With the end of bimetallism but with silver still being coined, legislation

---

[40] Timberlake, *Constitutional Money*, 14–15.

forced on the Congress by public agitation had it that any citizen could present the Treasury with another metal, silver, get a redeemable federal banknote for it, and demand gold for the notes. The notes could go on about how the Treasury could choose the redemption coin (gold or silver), but the Treasury found that if it did not redeem the notes in gold on demand, the markets would panic. In dropping bimetallism but still accepting silver, if limiting the total amount, Congress was, strangely enough, giving everyone one of the central powers of being a national bank. This was the opportunity to present, in a silver holder's case—or to create, in a bank's case—something that the government or its agents had to redeem in gold.

Over the decades following 1879, it became clear that this was perhaps a mistake. Or was it, considering that the beneficiary was the government? There was profit in striking coins. Silver producers and the farming Populists petitioned Congress to require the Mint to coin (for profit) silver brought to it. William Jennings Bryan, the Populist rhetorician and "thrice a candidate for the presidency of the Republic," as H. L. Mencken put it, was the fiery advocate for "free silver." Free silver meant that no matter how much people brought silver to the Mint, it had to be monetized into dollars ultimately redeemable in gold. Congress obliged to various degrees, permitting upwards of millions of dollars per month in silver to be coined after 1879. This was when US currency and non-gold coin, for practical purposes, had to be redeemed in gold and gold only on demand.

Bryan made a famous speech attacking the gold standard. This was his "Cross of Gold" oration on accepting the Democratic nomination for president in 1896. He feared the nation's being "crucified" on a cross of gold because, he felt, there was not enough gold to justify the amount of currency needed to head off deflation, a scourge of debt-laden farmers.

Bryan had a point. Before 1861, anyone could bring silver to the Mint and get it coined. Now they could not, outside of the occasional limited programs from Congress. Bryan's hoped-for free silver, however, involved a major difference. In the prior arrangement, currency could be redeemed for gold or silver at the discretion of the bank and the Treasury. Now it had to be gold. Free silver in the 1890s could break the banks under the solitary gold standard, as it had not in the least under bimetallism. After the Civil War, only national banks were allowed to issue gold-redeemable dollars. Now every petty owner of silver could functionally do the same by bringing their silver to the Mint.

The federal government had recently proved this problem a real one. Two years after passing its most expansive silver-acceptance act since dropping bimetallism (the Sherman Silver Purchase Act of 1890), the Treasury let it be known that it was running out of gold and needed quite a large loan from private sources to prevent it from suspending redemptions. J. P. Morgan and others arranged for the gold loan, and the Treasury made it through.

The collateral effect, appallingly, was the Panic of 1893. The restriction in credit across the banking system owing to the extraordinary needs of the Treasury, as well as the threat to redemption caused by those needs, prompted withdrawals and shut the financing lines of the private economy. The economic depression of the 1890s, in lore associated with "capitalism," was unthinkable outside of the United States' replacing bimetallism with a gold standard (and the national bank system's having government-mandated inelastic reserves in the form of federal bonds). Workers got crushed—hence Bryan's popularity as the Democratic nominee. The Sherman Silver Purchase Act had authorized large, regular federal purchases of silver for conversion into federal notes that people demanded be redeemable in gold. Had the act reinstituted bimetallism (let alone freed up the banking system from the federal hand), there would have been no run on gold. Government price and system-management discrepancies were at the heart of everything. Some crisis of capitalism.

Furthermore, the United States had also increased the tariff. In 1890, Congress passed a "protective" tariff such that its duty rates were so high that they would result in more revenue if lowered. Such a tariff required further taxation to make up for the lost revenue, lowered real wages by increasing prices, and increased the cost of capital goods used in business formation and expansion. All these effects depressed the demand for money, contributing to the run on gold.

A privately organized monetary system such as can emerge with Bitcoin and cryptocurrency would surely have the flexibility to avoid semi-disasters like the Panic of 1893. A dominant monetary issuer and regulator (in this case, the government) can make mistakes—such as the tariff, the mass monetizing of gold-convertible silver without bimetallism, and restricting the issuance of bank notes—all while taking cues from a political power as opposed to a market feedback loop. If possessed of a not entirely enlightened dominant player, indeed one with the power to tax alternative currencies, a monetary system can lack the suppleness to respond quickly and appropriately to stresses as they arise.

If, for example, a new unit of account arose combining Bitcoin, gold, and the dollar, crises such as those of 1893 would lose their basis. The dollar used to be redeemable in silver or gold. Now it could be gold or Bitcoin. The important point is that Bitcoin and cryptocurrency herald a new era of monetary innovation, in particular through the transmission and transferability of stored value, similar to what past generations regularly enjoyed. In the decades after 1865, the United States was groping, via the heavy hand of federal regulation, for a banking system that provided good currency equal to the great public demand of the peak years of the Industrial Revolution. Why not have a diverse private sector give monetary innovation a whirl? Tying currency creation to federal bonds after the war was odd. Federal debt was to go down after the Civil War because of demilitarization. The absence of further federal spending initiatives in peacetime, moreover, spurred on the enthusiasm for private enterprise. A national banking system based on federal bonds in such an environment was necessarily going to get stretched thin when it came to issuing currency equal to the public's level of demand. In view of such precedents, whatever might develop in terms of elastic cryptocurrency in our age, any reliance on government bonds as the basis for monetary issuance surely will be called legitimately into question.

This does not mean governments will have to relinquish major currency powers if Bitcoin and cryptocurrency become ascendant in the global monetary system. As lay political economist Henry George suggested to immense readership in the 1870s, governments can successfully confine themselves to issuing currency through procurement. If governments believe their currency is essential for the marketplace, then governments should create it as they buy things, replacing the tax system. Creating money and getting value for it is called "seigniorage." If governments believe they should create currency, this undermines the argument that those governments should also lay taxes.

Eliminating taxation in favor of Georgist government-money production through procurement would probably prove a powerful competitive challenge to Bitcoin and cryptocurrency. An economy that drops its tax system sports enormous increases in its after-tax returns to enterprise. In the United States, as of the early 2020s, the top tax rate stood at just about 40 percent. Such a rate leaves 60 percent of any profit stream as income. Eliminating taxation would increase the returns to marginal income by two-thirds, or 40 divided by 60 (as well as scramble current planning based on risk-return ratios). An exceptional wave of risk-taking and entrepreneurialism would sprout in such a context. The federal government would keep doing everything it had been doing by spending newly created dollars. Demand for dollars would soar because their income streams would be untaxed, forcing Bitcoin and crypto to compete as alternatives to a desirable government fiat dollar. Inflation would not emerge in such a currency and tax regime. The increase in the supply of goods and services on the elimination of taxation would be disinflationary.

Perhaps such notions sound fanciful. George was deadly serious as he outlined his proposals, and it remains difficult to overstate George's popularity across the economic classes in the United States and beyond during the Gilded Age. *Progress and Poverty* (1879), George's central book on economics, was, the Bible excepted, perhaps the bestselling book of the latter nineteenth century. Such popularity is a clue that reform of the dollar of this nature—which Bitcoin and crypto are calling forth in the twenty-first century—is consistent with deep-seated monetary attitudes and preferences of the democratic public.[41]

The Panics of 1819, 1873, and 1893 corresponded intimately to the insufficient attempts of the federal government to manage its own recent suspensions of classical monetary standards. In 1819 and 1873, the enormous increase in paper dollars after taking the dollar off gold and silver during wars was the issue. Thomas Mellon noted this point precisely. In 1893, the problem was dealing with the strange decision to demonetize a classical final-money precious metal, silver, while at the same time keeping the national banking system in a federal-bond straightjacket and not taking care to keep the demand for money robust by lowering taxation. In each case, necessarily, the banking system had to seize up until the problem was worked out, including making sure that federal finances were set up for the duration.

None of this had anything to do with innate instability in a banking system that issued currency redeemable the original way, in gold and silver coin. None of this had anything to do with instability in the industrial economy. None of this points in any rigorous way to a crisis of capitalism. These events were crises of governmental money and governmental regulation of money. Whatever brave new world Bitcoin and cryptocurrency have in store, it is unlikely that developers of a new monetary order in the twenty-first century will retrace the mistakes made in making money inelastic when it was demanded most, such as during the peak years of the American Industrial Revolution.

---

[41] On George, see Christopher William England, *Henry George and the Crafting of Modern Liberalism* (Baltimore: Johns Hopkins University Press, 2023).

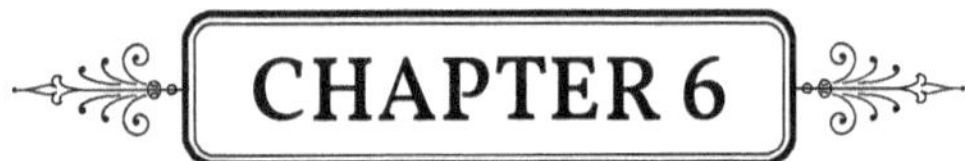

CHAPTER 6

Here Comes the Fed

The years of the gold standard/national bank system from 1879 to 1913 were a period of tremendous economic growth and the extension of opportunity—not least to the immigrants that poured into the nation by the millions. Nonetheless, the impression was never far from the surface in this period that political-economic arrangements were headed toward the brink. The deflation of the 1880s, the free-silver movement, Bryan and the Populists, and the Panic of 1893 and then one in 1907 contributed to the sense that the gold/national bank system had not set things just right—and that another monetary reform was in order. A reform came about with the creation of the Federal Reserve in the aftermath of the 1907 event.

The Panic of 1907 was a drop and recovery in the markets and in economic activity, complete with the failure of several central financial institutions, over the fall of that year and early the next. The causes remain difficult to ascertain. The San Francisco earthquake of the year before had occasioned enormous insurance claims (in part a result of poor federal land-rights policy, as in 1837 and 1857). The Treasury had also mismanaged how many of its own bonds it was making available for holding in the national banks, limiting the free issue of currency on the part of those banks. Why the federal government was still requiring its own bonds as the better part of the reserves of the national banks is an odd one. The United States had been running budget surpluses for decades. The national debt was going down, in nominal terms. In terms of the size of the economy—the relevant criterion for the banking system—it was plummeting. How was this diminishing thing supposed to "back" the banks serving the prodigiously growing greatest economy in the world?

Treasury secretary Leslie M. Shaw had started, during his time in office from 1902 to early 1907, to loosen federal restrictions on the national banks. He permitted non-Treasury-bond collateral against government deposits and relaxed federal mandates on reserve requirements, among other moves. Critics suggested that Shaw had set in place conditions for the panic. Richard Timberlake felt that if Shaw's efforts had been given a wider berth, the panic might have been averted:

> Another possibility that none of Shaw's critics ever addressed was the abolition of governmental controls and regulations over national bank currency and national bank credit operations…[A] policy of liberalizing national bank-note issues by releasing them from their rigid connection to government securities, abolishing legal-tender reserve requirements on national banks, and removing barriers to interstate branching would have given the banking

system the resiliency to cope with liquidity panics. Indeed, the financial upheavals that seemed to require Treasury intervention might never have occurred.

Timberlake further noted that throughout the Gilded Age, "the federal government monopolized the supply of all currency—gold, silver, U.S. notes, national bank notes, and silver certificates." Non-national bank currency not produced by the federal government was taxable and therefore nonexistent. National bank currency had to be based on a reserve ratio to US government bonds. If the federal government did not produce enough of such media—and government debt had been diminishing since 1865—or be flexible about reserve ratios, the national banking system it presumed to base on those media would have a supply and elasticity problem.[42]

The national banking system, that child of the Civil War, had at its heart a "fatal conceit," in F. A. Hayek's phrase. One national banking system with a largely uniform set of regulations of how much money its members could create on the basis of government debt ran the risk of making a big mistake. When there is one final arbiter of a system, it has to make good choices all the time. If it makes a mistake, there is no alternative arbiter to correct the mistake within the system. There is no corrective feedback loop. The one final arbiter has to have the "conceit" of believing it can readily make the best decision in each circumstance. In the case of the national banking system, the matter was even more muddied because the sole arbiter was diffuse. Congress, the Treasury, the growing office of the president—all sorts of federal powers had a hand in regulating the system of

---

[42]   Timberlake, *Monetary Policy in the United States*, 197, 210.

non-government, private national banks that issued the greater part of the whole of the nation's currency. Nobody clearly owned the problem within the federal government, should a problem arise.

The Bitcoin systems broadly starting to emerge in the twenty-first century resemble the aspirational structure of the pre-Civil War free-banking system more than the national banking system that followed it for some half a century. The pre-1861 free-banking system had its own burden in the form of state regulation and requirements to hold state bonds, the states having been desperados during their mass default period in the early 1840s. But, as the Suffolk arrangements and other innovations had proven, given a chance at developing the institutions of self-regulation, the private sector just might come through. Bitcoin and cryptocurrency are occasions to explore again opportunities in currency issuance that the United States had in its grasp in ages past but always seemed to choke off as things were getting interesting. In no period of United States history, given the brevity of the free-banking era (the state-chartered banking era might be the more apt term), were the potentialities of a private currency system given ample space and time to develop.

As for lenders of last resort, these existed to some perfection throughout the classical eras of American monetary history, including in the Panic of 1907. Such lenders were private entities called "clearinghouses." Clearinghouses emerged in the nineteenth century as a brake against systemic failure in the banking system. Clearinghouse associations were consortia of banks in a region. If banks in an association experienced a run, the members, on positively assessing the troubled banks' soundness, would rush money to them to stop the run. The IOU the banks gave in return was clearinghouse scrip acceptable among the association members. The resumption of good business after the forestalling of the panic enabled the borrowing banks to pay back the scrip IOUs with ordinary money. The national flagship was the New York City Clearing House. In 1907, this institution extended interbank scrip to nonmember trust banks facing the bulk of the runs. Technically, perhaps, this money was illegal—it should have been taxed like any non-national bank note. In 1908, Congress made it explicit that national banks could issue stabilizing scrip, unbacked by treasuries, to each other, in times of crisis.

The parallel to cryptocurrency again is palpable. Scrip is the prerogative of the crypto developer. One might even say that cryptocurrency, including Bitcoin, is scrip—it can be made and used according to the consensus of a community. To be sure, US dollars can be and are used as scrip in the broad clearinghouse sense—the bank bailouts of the early twenty-first century associated with the Federal Reserve quantitative easing programs, for example. But in the actual clearinghouse era over a hundred years ago, the point was to pay back the IOUs on the quick resumption of normal activities. The issuance of Federal Reserve scrip in contemporary times correlates instead to the making permanent of the conditions of secular stagnation. In theory, the quantitative easing (QE) programs were to function like scrip, even as the transaction medium (the dollar) was usable outside the banking community. QE, in theory, was to buy distressed assets, underwater mortgages and the like, hold them until they improved in value—until they were no longer "toxic," as the parlance went—and then sell them back into the market, retiring the currency. Yet the Federal Reserve's balance sheet remained bloated for eons after 2008—unthinkable in the efficient, quick-acting, and quick-resolving clearinghouse era. Private rediscovery of the virtues of the pre-Federal Reserve clearinghouse system is another intriguing possibility that Bitcoin, with its allied movements in cryptocurrency development, poses.

The origins of the Federal Reserve are recounted in thrilling fashion by G. Edward Griffin in his bestselling 1994 book *The Creature from Jekyll Island*. The island in question was the Georgia resort where a group of high financiers and politicians met in 1910 to plan the Federal Reserve. If one wishes a source besides Griffin, one can quote official Federal Reserve history:

> The meeting and its purpose were closely guarded secrets, and participants did not admit that the meeting occurred until the 1930s. But the plan written on Jekyll Island laid a foundation for what would eventually be the Federal Reserve System.
>
> At the time, the men who met on Jekyll Island believed the banking system suffered from serious problems....
>
> Like many Americans, these men were concerned with financial panics, which had disrupted economic activity in the United States periodically during the nineteenth century. Nationwide panics occurred on average every fifteen years. These panics forced financial institutions to suspend operations, triggering long and deep recessions.

Nationwide panics had been occurring every fifteen years: what a poor tribute to the Civil War national banking acts. To repeat yet again the Treasury's official history of those acts as of 2020:

> But the national banking system was also designed to achieve longer term economic goals.… Once accepting and holding national currency became essentially risk-free, it gained in public confidence and circulated throughout the nation. This represented a marked improvement over the pre-Civil War money supply.… Through the more orderly national money and banking system, Congress sought to promote economic growth and prosperity and a stronger sense of American nationalism.

It is difficult to imagine what such self-serving history could possibly be referring to. Where was this "more orderly national money and banking system," the absence of which, at least in perception, prompted the high financiers and politicians to the Jekyll Island huddle? Another way of considering the matter is to propose that the panics could have been, all along, functions of the overdone federal presence in monetary affairs. In any case, in 1913, here came the Fed.[43]

---

[43] "The Meeting at Jekyll Island, November 20, 1910–November 30, 1910," Federal Reserve History, Dec. 4, 2015, at www.federalreservehistory.org/essays/jekyll-island-conference.

A great inflation

Based on the planning undertaken at Jekyll Island and in a congressional National Monetary Commission that convened for several years after the Panic of 1907, in December 1913, three months after it approved the nation's first modern constitutional income tax, Congress passed, and the president signed, the Federal Reserve Act. Suddenly, over the last thirteen weeks of 1913, the United States had both an income tax and a Federal Reserve. Perhaps one of the reasons the states ratified the Sixteenth Amendment allowing the income tax is that the income tax would exempt interest from state and local securities—swelling demand for these instruments.

The Federal Reserve largely, but not completely, replaced the national banking system. Under the new arrangements, the national banks still existed and could still issue untaxed United States dollars. But they were now required, and the other banks invited, to keep their reserves not with each other but with the Federal Reserve. By the mid-1930s, about 80 percent of deposits were in member banks of the Federal Reserve. There were twelve Federal Reserve district banks, each theoretically corresponding to an economically distinct region, spread over the country.

Several important changes came with the Federal Reserve. The first was that United States bonds became less important in terms of guidance to the banks about how much currency and credit they could issue. The twelve Federal Reserve banks increasingly looked kindly on IOUs to depositors from commercial clients ("real bills" in banking parlance) as a basis for their member banks' lending. Also, the Federal Reserve itself began issuing national currency, the Federal Reserve Note, the currency of the United States that persists to this day. Now there were two forms of national currency: that of the national banks and that of the Federal Reserve. These notes, these US dollars, had a common design. The only difference was the markings indicating their institution of issue. All of them were redeemable in gold, to any holder, at the place of issue at the longstanding rate of $20.67 per ounce.

The base year of the consumer price index (CPI), which began to be developed in 1919, is 1913. Prices that year were the index number 10. As of 2021 (prior to the inflation takeoff of 2022), the CPI stood at 271. What it took ten dollars to buy—eggs, milk, apartment rooms, whatever the selection of representative goods—in 1913, as of 2021 it took $271. Another way of putting that is that a $100 bill bought 3.7 cents' worth of goods. The base year of 1913 makes sense because prior to that point, prices hovered around a par. The base of 10 prevailed for the long period before the creation of the Fed. Extrapolations back to 1815 show deflations and inflations here and there, at most outside of the Civil War amounting to a little over 20 percent (or plus or minus all of 2 in the CPI), with a return to the par of a CPI at 10 always achieved. For its part, the Civil War perhaps saw a 110 percent inflation (CPI of 22), with a recovery of the CPI par of 10 again by 1879.

As the twelve Federal Reserve banks were set up across the country in 1914, the CPI held at 10, as it did again in 1915. In 1916, it started going up. It has never neared recovery of the 1913 par. By the 1920s, the CPI was at 17; in the 1930s, it hung around 14; in 1945, it was 18; in 1955, it was 27; in 1965, it was 32; in 1980, it was all the way up to 82, and it surpassed 270 in 2021. Another way of thinking about this march of numbers is in terms of dollar devaluation. It took twenty-seven times the amount of dollars to buy the same goods in 2021 compared to 1913. The dollar experienced a 1-(1/27), or a 96 percent, devaluation against consumer prices over this long Federal Reserve era period.

And yet, one should be careful about associating all this with the Federal Reserve. The Federal Reserve's fingerprints appear to be all over the chronic inflation/devaluation of the 110 some years after the creation of the institution in 1913. Temporally, the correspondence is perfect. It is eminently reasonable to ask, in view of the huge secular inflation of the post-1913 era unprecedented in American history, *What Has the Fed Done To Our Money?*—a twist on the title of the 1963 Murray Rothbard book, *What Has Government Done to Our Money?* Clearly, the dollar as a store of value has been all but ruined.

Setting aside the interesting specifics of Rothbard's argument in that book, the title draws an important distinction pertinent especially to the early years of the Fed. The creation of the Federal Reserve made confusing yet again who claimed responsibility for the management of the money and currency system of the country. Under the pre-Fed national banking system, and for all its faults, it was generally the Treasury that took responsibility for its superintendence. Now the Fed was the main superintendent. In a crucial development, this decoupled the definition of the dollar from the increasingly preponderant federal note-issuing institution. The Treasury defined the dollar, in gold, while the Fed authorized the making of money—soon enough (by 1935) arrogating all currency production to itself.

As the Fed, after 1913, authorized US dollar credits and note-issuance from its member institutions on the basis of various media, real bills, gold in bank vaults including its own, government debt, and the like, it left dollar-definition policy to the Treasury. The Treasury said the dollar was 1/20.67 an ounce of gold. The Fed accepted this definition implicitly, but it was on a course of coming up with an alternative definition of the dollar, indeed, one that we have today (an alternative definition not voted on and with no record of a popular consensus, despite our democratic-republican form of government). This was that a dollar is that which the Fed issues as a dollar. In the Coinage Act of 1792, Congress looked around at the actual secular world of monetary transactions and found that an ounce of silver corresponded to a certain value in the goods and services transactions and made this the definition of the dollar. Once the Federal Reserve was established, a process got underway whereby the Federal Reserve's mere issuance of the dollar overcame all other definitions of the dollar. The Fed dollar became, if not fully by the 1930s then certainly by the termination of all elements of the gold standard in the 1970s, the dollar.

Once again, the market-competitive, private characteristics of Bitcoin and cryptocurrency present an alternative to this kind of monetary declaration, or "fiat" (a Latin term for a declaration). The monetary system of a specie-defined dollar governed the long heroic era of American economic growth from the late eighteenth through the early twentieth centuries. Then the Fed came to arrogate to itself the definition of the dollar, as economic growth rates fell markedly for the long term—a constant topic of the upcoming chapters—as chronic inflation became a fact of life, and as savers had to resort to taking on more risk to store the value of their work not in money per se but in speculative investments in stocks, real estate, and beyond, the mitigation via diversification yet another deadweight loss. The introduction of alternative private money and currencies via Bitcoin suggests the coming of alternative private monetary systems that aspire through competition to displace the fiat Fed dollar. It is important to note that the homely matter of defining money—a weight of specie, classically—had always been a feature of the American currency system until the rise of the Fed and the ultimate departure of any thought of offering a definition of money.

Nevertheless, the rise of the big new tax system, also beginning in 1913, has to have been central in the long crisis in monetary devaluation and definition that has plagued the country's economy, essentially unremittingly, since 1913. The income tax also begun in that year has, outside of only its first four years through 1916, featured a top rate on high earners that at its lowest has been moderate but typically has been objectively immoderate. The top progressive rate of the income tax was 77 percent in 1918 and stayed above 50 percent through 1923. Stewards of capital—the highest earners—had to see over half of their marginal profits and incomes sail off to the government if they played it by the book (which is to say, if they did not shelter their income from taxation, of which there was ample legal opportunity, a political spoils system masquerading in guises of equity and allocations toward public goods). Top rates were at the moderate level of 24–25 percent briefly, from 1925 to 1931. But after that, for five decades, the top rate was never below 63 percent. Since 1987, the top rate has generally hovered just below 40 percent.

The point with respect to the monetary system is that this big income tax acted as a major suppressant to the demand for money at the point of currency and credit creation, the banks, including the Federal Reserve. High earners and the rich by definition have the most money, the most assets, and the most robust income streams, and thereby the best and most ready collateral to acquire a bank loan. For example, before he started selling his Tesla shares in 2022, plutocrat Elon Musk apparently financed his consumption through bank loans. He staked Tesla stock as collateral at the bank and got the best terms on loans to buy his houses and other consumption items. He did this, clearly, because of the capital gains and the income tax. If he had sold shares to fund his day-to-day expenses, he would have faced capital gains taxes inclusive of California's running to 40 percent. Had he taken a commensurate salary, that salary would have faced income taxes again inclusive of California's topping 50 percent. His loan interest was not taxable, but deductible from taxable income.

An income tax system, such as the United States gave itself in 1913, will curtail the demand for money, namely bank credit, especially as that system is progressive in its rate structure and its top rates high. If people with money want even more for an entrepreneurial project or to expand a current operation (as when Musk borrowed money to buy Twitter), they are precisely the candidates the bank holds in highest regard because they have collateral. The bank will take the collateral and create new money and credit on the basis of that collateral for a good price, as the loan. Whenever tax rates are high and progressive, however, the rich sour on new entrepreneurial ideas and investments because of the taxes on the profits, the return. They approach the banks less for money. High progressive tax rates curtail—indeed they can kill—the demand for money in an economy.

This has next to nothing to do with the Federal Reserve per se. But it has everything to do with the depreciation of the currency. In the marketplace for any good or service, the strength or weakness of demand is a central determinant of the price. Generally, prices rise under strong demand and fall under weak, each move softened by the ability of supply to respond to the changes in demand. In the case of the dollar, the income tax sharply cut down the demand for it, as new issuance, from the banks. The price of the dollar had to fall, and supply should have fallen too. One way of saying that the price of the dollar fell was that all other prices went up. It took less and less of any good or service to buy a unit of money after 1913. If a dozen eggs fetched ten cents in 1913, the carton fetched 271 cents in 2021. The inflation of the post-1913 era meant that the price of the dollar fell against everything the dollar might be used to buy.

For the Federal Reserve to have perfectly managed the money supply in a new condition of money-demand suppression—the fruit of the progressive income tax—would have been a banking accomplishment for the ages. For all the criticism the Fed has come in for over the years, hanging the huge post-1913 inflation on it is, in significant part, to improperly exonerate a major culprit: the income tax. In an important sense, even a maximally enlightened and efficient Fed could not have staved off the inflation. If the stewards of capital, the rich and high earners, want money less because of progressive income taxation, they will want alternatives to money more, namely goods and services, and alternative assets, particularly non-financial ones, of all varieties as well. Prices will go up, no matter how the money supply replies to money demand. This is not to mention the imposition of other barriers to the monetary demand of the rich that arose mightily after 1913, including regulation and government spending, the latter of which, among other things, corrals the workforce otherwise available to the private sector into government employment and contracting.

Bitcoin and cryptocurrency offer no direct alternative to the national tax system. On tax matters, the main concern of Bitcoin entrepreneurs and the broad crypto community is that transactions in these new media become untaxable. Currently they are taxable—as a capital gain. If one acquires Bitcoin at a certain price and then uses it to buy something, whatever the price the Bitcoin fetches in that transaction becomes, before the federal tax code, the selling price of the capital asset of Bitcoin. If it is greater than the acquisition price, it must be reported for capital gains taxation and the tax paid. If a loss is involved, the deduction from other income is limited. The community greatly desires that such taxes on crypto transactions for goods and services (not to mention assets) be eliminated, as they are for transactions in the dollar. One does not have to assay the value of the dollar when it was acquired to determine the cost basis for when it is used to buy groceries at the store every day—this would be a ludicrous burden on the population. Crypto is asking for the same tax treatment of its transactions. The tax rule on this matter currently has been made by a bureaucrat, somebody no one has voted for.

Indirectly, Bitcoin and cryptocurrency offer a rather serious challenge to the tax system. Bitcoin and crypto rather plainly aspire to advance an alternative monetary system to the current one dominated by the fiat Fed dollar. The Fed can confront this alternative via hard or soft power. Via hard power, the allies of the Fed in government can make illegal, tax, and otherwise make life difficult for crypto on a legal level. (This is not to delve into the matter that constitutional grounds for anything beyond complete openness to Bitcoin and cryptocurrency is probably lacking.) Such moves, however, can raise the price of the harried alternative. Gold sure has gone up as the United States began restricting its monetary use in the 1930s. If the government harries Bitcoin, surely a similar result will ensue.

Via soft power, alternatively, the Fed and its allies in government can seek to make the fiat Fed dollar naturally attractive to the public. A Fed crypto, or CBDC, "central bank digital currency," is not at issue here. (CBDCs are laughed at in the crypto demimonde for not having spontaneous attractiveness in the marketplace, as Bitcoin does.) Rather, if tax rates on dollar income streams are lowered, the demand for the dollar naturally will increase. Classical supply-side tax, regulatory, and spending reforms are probably the best route to suppressing interest in Bitcoin and cryptocurrency in favor of the current fiat. People will freely invest with the dollar and drive up demand for it, as before 1913, if the returns come back closer to in-whole to the investor.

Money and the Great Depression

During the Great Depression in the 1930s, both the gold/specie standard and national bank dollars came to an end in the United States. In 1933, President Franklin D. Roosevelt ordered Americans to surrender their gold, including federal coins, to Treasury officials at the official price of $20.67 an ounce in currency and non-gold coin. On collecting it all that summer, Roosevelt's administration began the process of melting most of it into bullion and stashing it away at a new place under construction—the United States Bullion Depository in Fort Knox. In addition, the Treasury collected national bank dollars for redemption in Federal Reserve Notes, which became the sole paper currency, outside of rare issues from the Treasury itself, of the country from that point forward. It remained illegal for Americans to own gold from the summer of 1933 until

1974. Money held in cash, aside from coins and the occasional Treasury note or certificate, had to be in Federal Reserve Notes.

The national banking system therefore concluded. Banks could still have federal as opposed to state charters, with respective regulatory requirements and inspection regimens, but the chief reason for creating the whole system back in the Civil War was now gone. The national banks came into being so that there might be a national currency—the US dollar issued only by federally chartered banks with US bonds in reserve. Under FDR, the Federal Reserve took the final steps to arrogate currency creation to itself.

The ludicrous number of bank failures in the early Great Depression, the lion's share in the years 1931–33 before FDR came into office, have justly sullied the reputation of the Federal Reserve. The Federal Reserve was supposed to strengthen the banking system, and not two decades into its existence, there was a spectacle of bank failures that the most vicious of nineteenth-century speculators could not have conjured up in their nightmares. Excuses for the Fed's performance in the early 1930s include such arguments as non-member banks failing at a greater rate than banks that were members of the Federal Reserve System. By and large, however, representatives and even cheerleaders of the Fed concede the point. Ben Bernanke, as a governor of the Federal Reserve, said in 2002 of the causes of the bank failures in the 1930s: "We did it."[44]

Nonetheless, and perhaps astonishingly enough, once again it remains a possibility that people have been too hard on the Fed. Never had the United States had a tax system like it did

---

[44] Ben S. Bernanke, "Remarks on Milton Friedman's Ninetieth Birthday," Federal Reserve Board, Nov. 8, 2002, at www.federalreserve.gov/boarddocs/speeches/2002/20021108/.

in January 1932. At that point, the tariff was easily the largest—and had the highest average rates—of any in the nation's history. Needless to say, tariff revenues were low. On top of that, there was also a large income tax, with rates stretching up to 63 percent on top incomes—another novelty. Never before had the United States had both a large tariff and a major income tax. These conditions only began to obtain in June 1930, when the excessive Smoot-Hawley tariff became law, and the country was in its seventeenth year of an income tax, at that point with a 25 percent top rate. A huge tariff plus a notable income tax was unique in 1930 and 1931. A huge tariff (actually made bigger by the deflation of 1930–32) plus a greatly expanded income tax redefined the uniqueness of the fiscal impress on the economy in 1932. Into the bargain, state and local property tax rates were the highest they had ever been in the early 1930s.

The demand for money fell precipitously in these circumstances. The rate of return on income gained from business enterprises went down because of the taxation. Therefore, people with money and assets wanted bank loans less and less. Not only did this make the banks less profitable and jeopardize their ability to pay depositors; it also meant there was increased demand for alternatives to currency and easily transactable money. When the profitability of transactions goes down, the demand for the medium best at making transactions goes down, in particular with respect to those media not as good at making transactions.

Here was the origin of the spike in demand for gold in the early 1930s. People went to the bank and asked—as was their prerogative given national bank and Federal Reserve Notes, not to mention as a free people—for the equivalent value in gold. In his 1971 book *Monetary Theory*, economist Robert Mundell drew a graph illustrating the demand for gold. It indicated that there were two major drivers of the demand for gold. The first is that in times of economic success, when people get rich, they like to hold all sorts of assets. One asset class is gold. Therefore, when lots of people get rich, there is increased demand for gold, if proportionately less and less compared to the range of assets. The second is that in times of economic distress, namely when profits are low or threatened, people want less of the kind of money useful for purchasing investments and making payroll. In these times, people want more of other kinds of money, the kind less useful in transactions, including gold. The latter was the phenomenon that came over the economy from 1930 to 1933. In the first case, the increase in the demand for gold correlates with economic growth. In the second case, gold demand and the gold price shoot up as growth flags.[45]

When everyone wants gold, and the currency is redeemable in gold at a fixed rate, the demand for all other goods and services in that currency necessarily goes down. A general deflation will develop in the economy when there is a gold standard and a large demand for gold. Indeed, from 1930 to 1933, the consumer price index went from 17 to 13, a fall of 25 percent or so. Because a number of the tariff duties were specified in dollars and cents, the real value of these taxes went up given the deflation—here was another tax increase depressing the demand for transactable money. Investments dried up because profits were taxed, and the cost of labor went up given two factors. First, wages that did not go down with deflation were increased costs to the employer; and second, wages had to increase to stay at

---

[45]   Robert A. Mundell, *Monetary Theory* (Pacific Palisades, Calif.: Goodyear Publishing Co., 1971), 80.

real levels for the employees to cover the costs of the tariff, let alone the expanded income tax of January 1932.

In economics jargon, the "reservation wage"—the wage employees demand for any sort of work, a wage that correlates to maintaining one's self or a household one is responsible for—increased because of the taxes of the early 1930s. Employers said forget about starting, expanding, or even maintaining a business with that kind of cost structure. Everybody barreled into the bank to get gold.

Perhaps the Federal Reserve could have stemmed this tide better than it managed to. Innumerable studies have been run on how the Fed could have provided further "liquidity" and so forth over 1930–33. But the point remains that the demand for money went down. How supplying more of it would have solved the problem is not clear. If a punitive tax system suddenly materializes, nobody wants money, depositors take money out of the bank, they get gold, and they divert themselves with other pursuits until the profit-making outlook improves. Moreover, the problem was international. Major countries instituted serious income taxes only in the 1920s. There was nowhere to turn if one really wanted to make an enterprise investment with an eye on take-home profits. Otherwise ambitious people quit the economy, withdrew their money from the bank, and went into gold. The Federal Reserve, as the aspiring supplier of money, could not address the core issue—the deflated demand for money.

It is important to note that the deflation of the 1930s differed from deflation under the conditions of economic growth. Given economic growth and the innovations in production and product distribution it entails, the price of all goods should fall because there are so many new alternative goods that are quite available. In the Great Depression, prices fell because people wanted to hoard money given its uselessness as an investment medium in a suddenly extreme tax environment.

Bitcoin and cryptocurrency offer a vision of an alternative monetary—not an alternative tax—system. But again, the two systems are intertwined in such a way whereby reform in one can force reform in another. The national-bank-note system only came about after 1865 because the federal government took a positive, hard-power step to get rid of competitors. It taxed all currency, even that availing itself of the definition of the US dollar that the government had always offered, that was not national bank US dollars. The legacy currency of the pre-1861 era did not die in the heat of market competition, but because of a specific regimen of taxation that the federal government came up with for the express purpose of eliminating US dollar alternatives that it did not prefer. Surely a major reason the government did this—setting aside the formal justifications about "providing stability to the banking system"—was to provide a market for its bonds. Once the government got big in the Civil War, it had reason to worry that there were few natural, ready buyers for its debt instruments.

The national currency, first of the national banks and then the Fed, provided ready demand for federal bonds. National bank dollars had to be based on such bonds on deposit (those requirements loosened as federal debt went down after 1865). This was the heart and soul of the system. It was US government-debt based. Bitcoin obviously has nothing in common with this. Bitcoin does not aspire to gain a foundation in federal bonds, a ludicrous proposition. Quite the contrary, Bitcoin and the cryptocurrency movement it launched are embarking, if vaguely and somewhat unconsciously at the present relatively early moment, on a project of rediscovering what money can be when its basis of issue does not lie in government bonds (as in the national bank dollars) or in the wisdom of a largely governmental institution (as in the Federal Reserve Note). The clearest like in American history is in the pre-Civil War money and credit systems.

In those systems, the United States ideally confined itself to two humble monetary tasks. The first was offering a definition of a dollar (an ounce of silver at a ratio to gold) of which private people and institutions could avail themselves in the economy if they wished to. The second was setting up an explicitly profit-making business (namely the Mint) to compete with others from the private sector in making and striving to sell money in the market on this definition. As the government confined itself to these tasks, notwithstanding temporary expansions of federal monetary ambitions in the eras of the Banks of the United States, there was enormous monetary activity and innovation on the part of the private sector.

The Bank of Stephen Girard, the Suffolk system, and the free banks of the 1840s and 1850s (themselves typically having to deal with state governments demanding purchases of their debt as a condition of a charter)—extensiveness and variety characterized entrepreneurialism in the creation of money and credit as the United States prepped itself for leadership in the Industrial Revolution. This is the historical parallel that Bitcoin and cryptocurrency are outlining as they strive to develop in an era in which alternative monetary media to the officially produced dollar are still taxed, a legacy of the Civil War.

If the Fed and the government could summon the curiosity (by means of relaxing the tax and regulatory apparatus) to see what Bitcoin and cryptocurrency might produce on their own, the natural development might be a rapprochement among the legacy monies. Perhaps as things work out, the market might come to offer a definition of a currency unit, as in the Coinage Act of 1792. Perhaps it might bring together the two grand legacy monies with crypto. A unit of Bitcoin, a unit of the dollar, a unit of gold—this perhaps could function as the definition of a new general currency unit. Private parties—and governments too, if they wished to take part, in the spirit of the original Mint—would then offer new currencies in crypto or paper or whatever they like on the basis of this definition. These new currencies would be convertible in the base media.

Among the realizations that Bitcoin and cryptocurrency are pushing on the world is that governments themselves should strive to recapture their monetary soul. It used to be that governments saw their purpose, monetarily, as providing definitions of money and as a competitor in a marketplace as a producer of coin, if not currency. Today, governments have all but lost this sense of their own mission. They have central banks, currency, and regulations because the market is unstable and cannot produce such things on its own—badly invalid historical claims. Bitcoin and cryptocurrency are innovating in the broad monetary space, to be sure. An important aspect of this innovation is giving governments a chance to see again what they are best at when it comes to money.

CHAPTER 7

The Reserve Currency Era I: Bretton Woods

What the United States did with all the gold it confiscated from its citizens in the summer of 1933 is an odd story and caused misapprehensions about the nature of money and currency that have lingered to this day. Amassing who knows how much gold at $20.67 per ounce—the Treasury reported statistics at the time lowballing the number at some 3,000 to 5,000 tons—brought a whopping storage and security problem to the federal authorities. Where were they going to put this stuff, this gold, and what were they going to do with it?

The gold came in several forms. Beyond bars, the main form was US gold coins from over the years, umpteen eagles (ten-dollar pieces) and double eagles (twenty dollars), plus plenty of the smaller US coins that went down to $2.50. The vagueness of the order (it had a long run of fine print) did not banish the thought that people had to hand in extraneous jewelry too, if it was in excess of a personal gold hoard worth $100.

It seems—sources on this score remain preliminary—that the United States took in all of this stuff and boiled it, melted it down into bullion, and reshaped it into bars. Meanwhile, the government commissioned a vault for the ages to be built at a military base deep in the interior of the country, at Fort Knox in Kentucky. There the gold would sit, as the United States guarded it and contemplated its next steps. The bullion depository at Fort Knox opened—the *mot juste?*—in 1936.

The domestic hoard complete, the United States found itself amassing still more gold—from around the world. The international situation worsened badly as the 1930s wore on. The Empire of Japan invaded Manchuria (now northern China) in 1931 and China proper in 1937, Nazi Germany took over Austria and Czechoslovakia in 1938–39, and the Soviets and the Nazis helped themselves to Poland in 1939. If one has gold stored internationally—if one even is a central bank or a sovereign treasury—in such circumstances, one will want to shuttle one's gold out of the widening danger zone and into a safe haven. After 1936, the United States got all sorts of redemption requests from foreigners. These requests were not to redeem the dollar in gold, but the reverse. They were requests for the United States to provide a dollar for gold.

The gold confiscation of 1933 applied domestically. Americans had to hand over their gold that was in-country (in later years, the United States made clear that American citizens holding gold abroad had to hand that in too—as if Americans were subject to a dictatorship). The convertibility of the dollar to gold for foreigners remained in place. FDR variously suspended and changed the price of dollar convertibility to gold for foreigners over 1933–34. In 1934, he settled on thirty-five dollars per ounce as the foreign redemption price, with the dollar freely convertible to official foreign authorities.

At that thirty-five-dollar redemption price, gold flows from foreign sources for Federal Reserve Notes or dollar bank deposits came in at a huge pace, such that by the early 1940s, the United States probably held something like half of world monetary gold. The domestic confiscation of 1933, plus the foreign flows at the onset of World War II, yielded an official gold stock, on the part of the United States, the likes of which the world had never seen.

It was this development that began, or accelerated, a great regrettable unlearning about the relationship between gold and money. The subject of a previous chapter in this present book was the difference between the arithmetical increase in the amount of precious metal compared to the exponential increase in economic growth over the course of the Industrial Revolution. This divergence, as expressed in Newtonian calculus, justified fiat money that abided by a definition in final money (this is to "stretch" the definition of fiat money to include money defined in specie but far in excess of it). The fiat money corresponded to the exponential increase in economic growth, and the final money to the arithmetic increase in specie stocks. If fiat money had not expanded well past the levels of specie stocks, then the Industrial Revolution would have lost its financing instrument and probably come to a stop.

The central point is that the definition of all money was a weight of specie. Fiat money adopted that definition on the understanding that fiat money would come to dominate specie stocks given serious economic growth of any duration. The definition of fiat money in weights of specie ensured that the amount of fiat money corresponded to that which the economy needed to grow robustly. Whenever the public lost confidence in fiat money—or in economic prospects—in would come redemption requests. The key to warding off these redemption requests lay both in issuing only the amount of fiat money that an active private economy needed and seeing to it that there were no barriers (such as onerous taxation, regulation, or cronyism) to an active private economy. Again, "fiat" in this sense refers to convertible money far in excess of the metal-money base.

Fort Knox of the early 1940s occasioned quite different thoughts about how a currency should relate to its underlying definitional asset. Now it came to appear that an issuer of currency should "back" its currency in the reserve medium that it in fact had in its possession. The United States had a mother lode of gold, probably an outrider statistically in world history as the greatest ever (and therefore thrown out on relevance criteria), and it was the sole issuer of currency within its borders. Therefore, the amount of gold that a currency issuer has should correspond to the amount of currency that that issuer should put forth. Perhaps a percentage should be the rule—25 percent of currency outstanding should be in reserve in masses of gold.

This was not the relationship that had obtained when there were numerous issuers of currency—of the dollar—on a common definition. The relationship that obtained was that described by Jude Wanniski. A currency issuer put forth currency to their heart's content until the person on the margin showed up and started demanding gold over dollars. Here was the signal that the market had been satiated with currency. In this conception, there is no reference to the size of the gold stock the currency issuer has or to the collective size of gold stocks across issuers. There is only interest in the marginal demand for the reserve definitional asset over currency.

Moreover, Newton's arithmetic-exponential difference proved that given time—such as centuries—of an industrial revolution, the ratio between specie stocks and useful currency would continually shrink and become quite small. Therefore, the notion that gold should back a currency or that currency outstanding should reflect a constant healthy percentage of gold stocks held in reserve is incompatible with the monetary outlook that fostered the Industrial Revolution. Money is to be made usefully and efficiently like anything else in a product-rich industrial revolution. Declaring that it should not be made, even if people find it useful and efficient, ordinarily would be a mistake that other participants would quickly correct by making money that the one issuer had talked itself, incorrectly, into not making. But what if there is only one issuer, and that is the issuer that talks itself into having a reserve ratio in gold?

This was the problem that stalked Fort Knox and the American amassing first of domestic and then foreign gold in the 1930s and 1940s. The dollar float should be a function of how much gold the United States has: a new idea in the long era of the Industrial Revolution, dating back to Newton two centuries prior. As financial historian James Grant has noted concerning British currency issuance in the nineteenth century, gold was the "Old Maid," as in the Victorian card game. Nobody wanted to be the one holding it, because that was the medium one had when refraining from making investments. In an investment-rich environment, one wants to be a participant, not sitting out.[46]

The United States of the Great Depression was, however, not an investment-rich environment. This unpleasant fact

---

[46] James Grant, *Bagehot: The Life and Times of the Greatest Victorian* (New York: Norton, 2019), 52.

brought about more misplaced support for the idea that Fort Knox gold should back the dollar. In the 1930s, private demand for the dollar was abysmal. The deflation against the gold standard in the early 1930s proved the point. So did the New Deal. The public works programs consistently employing three million individuals in the latter 1930s (probably the worst era of the Great Depression) indicated that private demand for new money to make payroll and expand business was horrid. On the margin, people would prefer gold to money, if that option had still existed in the United States after 1933. The slack demand for money during the whole of the Great Depression was the necessary precondition for entertaining the idea that a huge gold stock, such as that at Fort Knox, should govern the absolute amount of currency outstanding.

If there had been good private economic growth in the latter 1930s, a recovery that blew far past ex-government GDP levels of 1929 for instance, there would have been no reason to suppose that the level of the American gold stock should determine the amount of currency. The amount of currency would have been galloping, given the growth, leaving the gold hoard (even if increasing) ever further in the dust. The criterion of marginal redemption requests would have held. Historically, it had been suspicious and dodgy currency issuers (such as Imperial Russia) that amassed, as sovereigns, large gold stocks to create the impression of a good currency. Conceivably, a currency under a gold standard should be more desirable the less its issuer holds gold in reserve. This would be a strong signal that the public at large finds this currency to be judiciously issued.

The concern that Bitcoin has a final quantity (of 21 million), and therefore would fail as a currency medium because of quantitative insufficiency, is to fall into the Fort Knox trap.

Bitcoin is not necessary to cover ever-increasing transactions in a growing economy with an evolving hybrid crypto/legacy fiat/gold monetary system. Gold never played this role in the Industrial Revolution. Bitcoin's status as the foundational cryptocurrency, along with its quantity and extraction limitations, confer to it gold-like characteristics. It is likely to be a final, redemption-request form of money, as specie of yore in the era of the Industrial Revolution. Other money, other crypto and other fiat monies defined perhaps in Bitcoin (and in gold as well), will be those lent out and otherwise produced to finance future economic growth. The view that Bitcoin has insufficient and deflationary characteristics is mistaken, an intellectual legacy of the Great Depression, when money demand was so poor that it gave rise to musings about absolute levels of gold needed to base a currency. An ambitious people should not take their positive lessons from the Great Depression.

Gold drain

The dollar stayed un-demanded for private economic purposes, and Fort Knox filled, as the United States successfully prosecuted World War II over 1941–45. The United States was aware, however, that once peacetime came, the private economy would seek to take over its natural role as the predominant force in commerce, enterprise, and employment. Demand for valid currency was coming. What to do given the huge gold stock and the fiat Federal Reserve dollar?

At the Bretton Woods conference in New Hampshire in July 1944, representatives of forty-four nations discussed and ratified an American plan to base the postwar world currency system on Fort Knox. The plan, implemented in phases after the war, was for the dollar to be defined and redeemable in gold at the current thirty-five-dollar-per-ounce price. Other countries had to maintain fixed exchange rates to the dollar, or to currencies fixed to the dollar. The criterion was 1 percent moves in the private markets against the exchange-rate par. If there was more than a 1 percent movement, countries could call on the International Monetary Fund (IMF) to help them get back to par. The IMF was a Bretton Woods creation. Its purpose was to be a dollar-flush exchange-rate-stabilization fund. If countries saw their currencies slipping against the dollar, they could use their IMF quota of dollars to buy their currency and get the prevailing exchange rate within the narrow band.

The dollar redeemable in gold on demand, at thirty-five dollars per ounce, to foreign authorities and fixed exchange rates otherwise—this was the plan as the soon-to-be victors of World War II contemplated the implications of peacetime in 1944. As Robert Mundell noted, Bretton Woods changed little in practical terms. A disproportionately large American gold stock had been a fait accompli by 1934, the foreign flows augmenting it afterward. As of 1934, the world realized that the dollar was becoming the paramount currency, and that any other currency's exchange rate in terms of the dollar determined that currency's value in general. Bretton Woods blessed the international currency arrangements that had come about in the maelstroms of the Great Depression and World War II. The articles of agreement of the IMF allowed countries to make an independent fix to gold, but nobody did. The size of Fort Knox intimidated everyone into fixing to the dollar.[47]

---

[47]   Robert A. Mundell, "A Reconsideration of the Twentieth Century," *American Economic Review* 90, no. 3 (June 2000), 332.

As the system got going after the war, countries generally shrunk their government sectors. Federal spending in the United States, for example, went from 41 to 11 percent of GDP from 1945 to 1948, as the Republicans took Congress in a landslide. West Germany, Japan, France, and Italy each arranged for modest government profiles against the private economy in comparison to the high marks of the crisis years of the 1930s and early 1940s. Each of these countries grew well, with Japan and West Germany becoming the second and third largest economies in the world, respectively, by 1965. Great Britain was the growth laggard. Its fiscal priority after 1945, as it soon became the biggest Marshall Plan recipient, was industry nationalization.

Large private-sector economic growth after World War II meant that demand for currency was strong. This was the major reason for the success of the Bretton Woods arrangements. The diminished profiles of governments in the economy offered a large field of opportunity for entrepreneurs and business expansion. And because of the fixed-exchange-rate mandate of the monetary system, investors bid for money to start and expand enterprises, confident that currency devaluations would not occur. Countries generally had little trouble keeping to their pars against the dollar.

The United States began to fret, however, that its gold stock was diminishing given the big global economic expansion. How could the United States guarantee—how could it "back"—the dollar in gold if the Fort Knox mother lode stayed the same in size while worldwide demand for currency redeemable in dollars, and hence gold, increased at the healthy clip of post-war economic growth? Year by year, in the 1950s and into the 1960s, the United States faced net positive foreign redemption requests of the dollar into gold. Fort Knox was being depleted.

In an important sense, this development was natural and welcome. A major reason the United States' gold stock had been so large to begin with was the huge foreign inflows under the conditions of war. With a good run of peace, as other places got rich, the natural inclination to balance portfolios with an element of gold meant that the United States would recycle the gold back into the world via redemption requests. But in another sense, constant demand for American gold reflected sagging demand for the dollar. President John F. Kennedy was clear on this point when he justified his series of tax-rate reductions, in the early 1960s, in terms of attracting dollars from abroad given an enhanced after-tax rate of return in the United States.

The tax-rate reductions notwithstanding, the United States preoccupied itself, in the 1960s, with devising petty fixes to the "gold drain." It encouraged an "incomes policy" whereby major industries and unions would agree to slow wage growth. If wages did not surge ahead, the theory went, there would be no "cost-push" pressure among producers to raise prices. Less inflation in the United States would make the dollar preferable to foreigners otherwise contemplating exchanging for gold. The federal government imposed an "interest equalization tax" on Americans' purchases of foreign financial securities. It established a "credit restraint program" that offered "guideposts" (the incomes policy had guideposts too) to companies, showing them how to limit their investments abroad. It encouraged military families in Europe and Asia to spend their dollars on base. It entreated Americans to limit foreign travel. The drumbeat of these initiatives in the 1960s was continual. The less that dollars went abroad, care of all this, the less the level of foreign claims on the gold stock.

The efforts were all in the name of stemming the gold drain from the original American mother lode, from Fort Knox. Here was a monetary theory that the currency issuer's own stock of the definitional asset of the currency had fundamental systemic significance. This notion was unknown during the period of the Industrial Revolution prior to the Great Depression and World War II. No Suffolk bank concentrated on claiming it had a huge percentage of gold coin on hand to back its currency issuance. If it made noises in this direction, surely holders would have rushed to redeem the currency. A bank publicly hoarding gold would appear to be one fearing a run. Banks in good health wanted more gold to make more loans, not to apparently strengthen a book ratio for some regulator.

No post-Civil War national bank—superintended by the federal government no less—would have advertised its gold stock or, for that matter, that of the system as a whole. The basis of the money, the "backing," was federal bonds. William Jennings Bryan should have said, in 1896, that American prairie poor folk were being nailed not to a cross of gold, but to a cross of federal bonds in national bank reserve accounts. At any rate, over the 1870s–1890s, dollars kept getting more competitive against gold (there was deflation) because the investment environment was excellent. At the margin, it was clear that people wanted dollars more than they wanted gold. The total size of a bank's or the system's gold stock was not an important issue. Without question, the ratio of the economy's size, and therefore the notional money supply, to the aggregate stock of gold was widening.

The mentality of the late Bretton Woods period, as the 1960s wore on, came from different suppositions. Now the stock of gold mattered. Again it must be stressed that an emphasis on the issuer's stock of gold derived from the extraordinary events of the Depression and the war. The United States confiscated Americans' gold in 1933 and then beheld foreigners offering the better part of their own gold to the United States. The amassing of official American gold over 1933–44 was a result of crisis politics. The novelty of the United States having a surpassingly large gold stock as of the Bretton Woods conference in 1944 somehow did not communicate itself as such. A quarter-century later, the presumption among policymakers and other constituencies (corporations loved wage-suppressing incomes policies) was that the absolute size of the American gold stock mattered. It was this concern that hastened the abrogation of the gold standard—for good, as it turned out—in 1971.

Bitcoin rather advertises that its stock is limited. Even now, it is pushing its final upper bound. Of the 21 million total Bitcoin ultimately minable, 19 million already exist. The coin may be finely divisible (up to the eighth decimal point), but gold, the seventy-ninth element on the periodic table, has similar characteristics. Bitcoin perhaps is more absolutely limited than gold. We have no complete idea of the final stock of gold. Unexpected strikes can happen at any time and increase our estimation of the total potential stock of gold.

Bitcoin does not support claims that the absolute amount of definitional money must determine the money supply, the amount of currency outstanding, or some good percentage of transactable money made in its name. In its ostentatious presentation of itself as of limited quantity, Bitcoin is offering an opportunity for a great relearning of old monetary verities. The interregnum of a national-gold-stock monetary system of the mid-twentieth century was just that, an interregnum. Before the 1930s, and certainly before World War I, few thought in these terms as the Industrial Revolution proceeded in its glory. After 1971, once again, few thought about national gold stocks having fundamental systemic significance. This was because the United States went off gold, and no one dared go back on. What happened to the idea that final, definitional money had only marginal significance—to the idea that the marginal demand for that final money is what mattered?

Bitcoin's effective flaunting of its limits—19 of 21 million already mined, and 21 million is not a large number in these days of trillion-dollar deficits and market capitalizations—can prompt us to rediscover what the purpose of definitional money was before the twentieth-century convulsions and their aftermath. Useful aspects of monetary wisdom went by the wayside with the unusual epic catastrophes of the twentieth century. In the normal course of the Industrial Revolution, the stock of gold fell constantly, as a ratio against active money outstanding. Yet, from the 1940s on, the general understanding about gold has been that there is not enough of it to base a monetary system. Bitcoin aspires, perhaps in concert with gold, to base a monetary system—and there is not terribly much of it. In this paradox—a paradox only from the modern perspective—may lie the beginnings of new good, elastic, growth-spurring currency in the twenty-first century.

August 15, 1971

On Sunday evening, August 15, 1971, President Richard Nixon made a television announcement that the United States was "temporarily" suspending its payments in gold to foreign authorities as of the next morning's opening of the markets. Never again has the dollar been convertible in gold. This event has become known as the "Nixon shock." It made unnecessary all the petty attempts to save the American gold stock—the incomes policy, the credit restraint, interest-rate equalization, and keep-the-dollars-at-home programs, even though for the most part they persisted (as government programs do) for a number of years thereafter.

Why did the United States go off gold? This question is more difficult to answer than it may appear. It was, surely, a mistake to assume that the aggregate official gold stock of the United States should enter into assessments of dollar policy. Did the authorities permit such a mistake in judgment to direct their actions? Perhaps more real, truly fundamental forces were at work. Traditionally, specie standards and fixed rates of exchange (which specie standards make necessary) prevailed when nations, or currency areas, had similar fiscal profiles. In the nineteenth century, governments were far smaller than they came to be in the twentieth century. The federal government of the United States was normally 3 percent of GDP in the nineteenth century. It held past 15 or 20 percent even in peacetime in the twentieth. The income tax did not exist outside of trivial exceptions before 1913, but after that, it was constant. From 1917 on, top income tax rates were never below 24 percent.

Differences in fiscal profiles among currency-issuing countries prompt capital to flow accordingly. If the after-tax rate of return is higher in the United States than in France, capital will flow from France to the United States (as in the pretext for the interest equalization tax of the 1960s). For example, when France upped its new income tax in the 1920s while the United States cut its own, the franc plummeted against the dollar, reflecting capital flows. Under fixed rates of exchange, capital flows into a country will cause domestic inflation, and those out of a country, domestic deflation. The pressure is strong, in these circumstances, for countries going through either experience to change the fixed value of the currency to eliminate the inflation/deflation or to forsake fixed for floating exchange rates.

Arguably, this process—outlined in the exchange-rate economics of David Ricardo in the nineteenth century—is what broke the Bretton Woods gold standard. Top progressive tax rates had gotten very high across the industrialized world after World War II. This afforded enormous opportunity to alter a nation's terms of trade by lowering the rates. The United States lowered its top tax rate from 91 to 70 percent over 1963–65. This big tax-rate cut increased the rate of return of top income from nine to thirty cents on the dollar, a huge jump of 233 percent. Meanwhile, Britain's top tax rates held at 90 percent. The two countries were major trading partners. Inflation materialized in the United States. In 1967, notwithstanding the fixed-rate conventions of Bretton Woods, Britain devalued the pound sterling by 14 percent. Changes in the comparative after-tax rate of return on investments in each country resulted in capital flows that broke the fixed exchange rate.

West Germany and Japan, meanwhile, were experimenting with revaluing their currency. This is to increase a currency's exchange rate—in this case, against the dollar. The huge tax apparatuses, in particular large schedules of progressive income tax rates, gave countries opportunities to change their relative economic attractiveness drastically against trading partners. An increase or decrease in top tax rates would occasion capital flows, applying pressure on exchange-rate fixity. The dollar's fix to gold was the anchor of the system. As fiscal policy switched in the 1960s, the fixed exchange rate to gold felt the pressure of global investment preferences for that place, wherever it may be, that sported the best after-tax return.

It may simply be that gold and specie standards only work when countries' fiscal profiles are small and the opportunity to change them quickly and drastically for practical purposes does not exist—the world before 1914, the world we have lost. This is not necessarily an argument for flexible exchange rates. Given that specie standards and fixed rates accompanied the phenomenal Industrial Revolution the whole while—including in the glorious growth runs of the post-World War II prosperity—perhaps the point is to trim the profile and reach of fiscal policy, the more to enable specie standards and fixed currency exchange rates and the wonderful growth that accompanies them.

Once again, the future toward which Bitcoin is militating is apparent. Bitcoin's emulation of gold, and its nearly palpable self-presentation and self-conception of itself as the cult-like base money of the twenty-first century, suggests that fiscal policy and profiles are to bow to it, not vice versa. Bitcoin heralds a new era, suggestive of the pre-1914 period, of modest government fiscal and particularly tax profiles. If we are going to have base, conceivably fixed-rate money again, there cannot be enormous capital flows breaking the system all the time. This perhaps is the "stick" by which Bitcoin warns governments that they must get small. The "carrot" is the prospect of nineteenth-century levels of economic growth again, at long last.

The term "reserve currency" has enjoyed a revival in recent years. The United States basks in its reserve currency status. China, Russia, or other aspiring hegemons are trying to challenge the dollar's reserve currency status. Great Britain no longer enjoys the prerogatives of a country sporting a reserve currency. Often-heard points such as these, in contemporary political-economic and geopolitical discussion, make use of this term. Conventionally, "reserve currency" has had a narrow meaning in international finance. It refers to the denominational profile of the foreign exchange that a country's monetary authority or treasury ministry holds. A country's "reserves" are those liquid foreign financial assets, inclusive of currencies, that that country owns. A country's reserves are all such assets, in official accounts, that are not in that country's own currency.

In this conventional conception, all currencies are reserve currencies. Any country that trades with the world finds some minimum of its own currency in foreign accounts. Certain currencies will pile up more than others in foreign accounts, and foreigners will have preferences to hold one currency not their own over another. In this sense, certain currencies can be reserve currencies more than others. Nonetheless, currencies of all non-autarkic places must sit in reserve in some amount somewhere on the globe.

After the United States went off the gold standard in 1971, the major countries of the world forsook fixing their currencies to the dollar. Beginning in 1973 (and in most cases lasting to this day), major currencies "floated" or had "flexible" exchange rates against each other. Foreign exchange markets developed in which buyers bid and sellers asked for currencies at prices that these individual market participants saw fit. The exchange rate became whatever you got for a currency, in another currency, when you made the trade. The quotation of a foreign exchange rate was that of the last trade.

In such a context, prevailing after 1973, demand for the dollar in currency reserve accounts soared. The dollar had been the globally dominant currency since 1945. But under fixed exchange rates, the norm until 1973, other currencies were just about equivalent to the dollar, because they could be exchanged for a dollar at a rate that did not change outside of, by today's standards, exceedingly narrow margins (and despite the odd devaluation or revaluation). Countries maintained dollar reserves to ensure their currency's fix to the dollar in case a market depreciation happened. In that case, countries would use the reserve dollars to buy their own issue to get the exchange rate back up to the fixed rate. If they ran low on reserves, they borrowed against their IMF quota and paid the dollars back after the crisis lifted.

Once flexible exchange rates became the norm after 1973, however, countries had an acute new interest in accumulating exchange reserves. Because the prices of currencies could and did change at any time in the newly active and expanding currency exchange markets, a sharp and novel element of uncertainty accompanied every currency's exchange rate. If the French franc trades four for a dollar now, will it be six for a dollar next week? Under Bretton Woods, the general sense was that next week the currency would be worth exactly what it was in dollars at present. It dawned on countries that they needed far more currency reserves than before. If their currencies were subject to sudden, rapid declines in the flexible-rate currency markets, potential investors would have that much more reason to pause in making a capital commitment in that country, given that receipts and profits would come from such an investment in the currency in question. Countries needed large stashes of dollars, like never before, to intervene in the exchange rate markets to protect their currencies from major declines and volatility.

The reserves had to be in dollars. The dollar in the 1970s, as today, was the currency, far more than any other, in which contracts and accounts the world over were denominated. If you were doing business with someone globally, that person was likely to accept the dollar, more than any other foreign currency, for settlement. Therefore, when the goal was to stabilize an exchange rate—say, the franc-West German mark exchange rate—the country in question would prefer to stabilize its currency against the dollar. Then it would be stabilized against all other currencies in dollar terms.

Foreign currency reserves grew and grew, in a process essentially unabated to this day. The trading of currencies increased to a ludicrous degree. Today, currency trading is easily the largest market in the world. Something like $8 trillion per day globally is the turnover in the currency markets. Banks capture the arbitrage at the expense of real producers. For comparison, American stock exchanges average about $500 billion in turnover per day. Currency market turnover every three days and change is the size of the yearly GDP in the United States. The currency-trading market has grown at something like 10 percent per year over the last half-century, as the Bank of International Settlements in Switzerland strives and struggles to account for it. However one puts it, this is an Einsteinian level of exponential growth.

It is essential, in this context, to note that a country gains in exchange reserves only in one way—through international trade. A country cannot print money and get another's. That would devalue the exchange rate and defeat the purpose. A country gets dollar exchange reserves when its own currency holders bring dollars to the country's central bank or treasury and ask for local currency in return. Therefore, an increase in international trade and international investment is the necessary condition for an increase in the total stock of currency reserves.

Since 1971, world trade has increased mightily. International trade in goods and services increased nearly four-and-a-half-fold in real terms from 1970 to 2000, or 5 percent per year, comfortably above the global rate of economic growth of a shade over 3 percent. Another way of putting it is that growth in world trade, over that generation, was greater than world economic growth by about two-thirds. It could be that technology, communications, and management and business operations practices have so improved with respect to world trade that it increased at such a high rate for reasons of economic efficiency. The question is why then was economic growth so average—at some 3 percent—when world trade expanded so mightily in the generation after 1970?

It could be that the switch to flexible exchange rates and no gold standard introduced a powerful new demand for world trade. Countries needed currency reserves like never before. Up went world trade, the necessary condition for fulfilling that demand. From this perspective, the increase in world trade did not reflect the gains from trade classically outlined in the economics of David Ricardo: each country specializing in what it does best so everybody gets richer. Rather, it reflected the need to produce currency reserves for the flexible exchange rate system. To the extent that this process was in operation, the increase in world trade expressed an economic inefficiency. Trade went up to minister to the monetary system as opposed to the economy itself. The resources that went into accomplishing world trade were, to a degree, a deadweight loss—the cost of dealing with the requirements of exchange-rate flexibility. This interpretation is consistent with the fact that while trade went substantially up and currencies traded like never before after 1970, economic growth was unremarkable.

Bitcoin outlines an alternative to the flexible-rate international monetary regime under which the world has been laboring since the 1970s. Bitcoin does not imply flexible, but fixed exchange rates. In its emulation of gold, Bitcoin beckons toward the pre-1971 era in which a final money established the definition of currencies, or at least the major currency (in the Bretton Woods case, the dollar). Bitcoin, like gold, is not set up to be traded the likes of $8 trillion dollars' worth per day. Activity of that extent and of that value is remarkable in its not resulting in a final useful economic product. In the days of the gold standard and before that bimetallic currency definition, there was, by modern criteria, little interest in exchanging currencies for final money, so long as the private economy remained a productive realm of investment, transactions, commerce, and savings.

Differences in fiscal profiles of the major nations may well have broken the gold standard and fixed exchange rates in the 1960s and early 1970s. The alternative that arose as the *de facto* architecture of the international monetary system—flexible exchange rates and the massive accumulation of exchange reserves—proved to devour economic resources in a way classical monetary systems never had. Bitcoin and cryptocurrency, as they mature, are inviting the world economy to rediscover something lost in the last half-century in terms of the relationship of money to the economy. When money has a definition, typically implying exchange rate fixity, economic resources flow more naturally toward real purposes. When money lacks a definition, economic resources flow more naturally toward the unreal purposes of the processes of the monetary system. A world in which Bitcoin and gold define final money is one in which places will have to compete for good currency. Bitcoin also therefore heralds a decline in the fiscal profiles of the nations of the world—in favor of robust private-sector economic growth that is the basis of the demand for money in the first place.

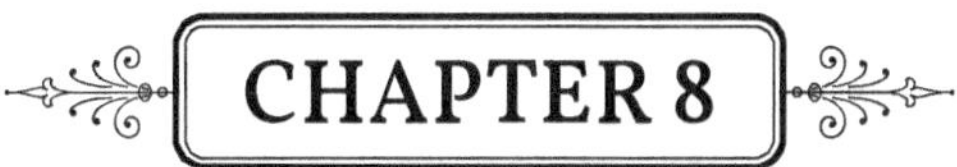

CHAPTER 8

The Reserve Currency Era II: Bitcoin Arrives

By any conventional standard, the economy of the initial years of flexible exchange rates, from the 1970s to the early 1980s, was not merely poor, but poor in an eccentric fashion. When flexible rates took over in 1973, an extended recession occurred, lasting until 1975, that was by most criteria the worst since the Great Depression of four decades before. The number of unemployed in the United States, for example, doubled from the previous norm of four million to eight million. The unemployment rate hit 9 percent, easily the highest since records began in 1948. And yet inflation totaled 30 percent, over 9 percent per year, over 1973–75. A nasty recession throwing people out of work was one thing. Such a recession coupled with enormous price increases was quite another. As people lost jobs and, with them, wages, everything there was to buy went up and up in price. Savings and investments got crushed against the dollar depreciation. The stock market at its trough in December 1974 was 40 percent off its nominal high of 1966, and well more than 50 percent in inflation-adjusted terms.

The recovery of 1976–78 saw 1960s-level real growth rates of 5 percent per year. But inflation was stubborn at 7 percent, many times higher than the 1-percent standard of peacetime in recent decades. Then 1979–82 outdid 1973–75. There were two recessions, unemployment crossed 10 percent, and inflation was in double digits for three consecutive years (1979–81). People called the extended post-1973 episode "stagflation"—economic stagnation coupled with big price inflation.

Stagflation in the 1970s and early 1980s was a precondition for Bitcoin. The immediate result, at the outset of flexible exchange rates and no gold, was this new, weird, unpleasant economic experience. Stagflation was proximate to, and the correlate of, the final doing away with definitional money in general and the gold standard in particular. Debate proceeds about the causes of stagflation. It came from the oil shock, labor union pressures, Vietnam and Great Society budgets, and foreign competition—all these are standard entries in the debate.

No space, however, separated the ending of gold and fixed rates and the depreciation of the dollar. The depreciation came immediately afterward. When the gold anchor got ditched, on came inflation. The switch in the monetary system in the early 1970s concerned how currency issuers regarded the definition of their issues. Before this period, the issuers abided by a definition. Afterward, they did not. Inflation ticked up as the possibility of the switch came on the horizon in the late 1960s and early 1970s and then became epochal once the switch occurred after 1971–73. Mass dubiousness about what an economy's money is worth is the essence of inflation. It is precisely this that the departure from remnant classical money in the 1970s prompted.

The public despised the Great Inflation of the 1970s. The embarrassment of stagflation is on the record of the official move to non-classical, to pure fiat, money. The public found stagflation outrageous, and that public was not to be fooled again.

Soon after stagflation bounded into the 1980s, quite abruptly a long, smooth, disinflationary economic expansion occurred. From 1982 to 2000, the economic growth rate typically approached or exceeded 4 percent per annum, while inflation, the scourge of the previous era, fell markedly to about 2–3 percent annually for the long term. The number of jobs in the United States increased by some forty million. Economists at one time were pleased to refer to this expansion as the "Great Moderation."

The President Ronald Reagan and Bill Clinton eras, the 1980s and the 1990s, recorded fantastic economic statistics and left stagflation in the dust. But in those years, no leader made any move toward reinstating classical money. This was peculiar, in that the departure from classical money had occasioned stagflation in the 1970s and sustained it the whole while through the early 1980s. Reagan defeated stagflation, and Clinton kept it down. But both presidents did so without addressing themselves to monetary reform, which was the root problem.

The public sensed this and remained partly enthusiastic and partly dubious about the economic sensations of the 1980s and 1990s. The growth, disinflation, increase in wealth, and start-up business culture were great. The mass layoffs (if complemented by ample net job growth), young adults moving all over the place away from their families in search of changing opportunities, and the sharp increase in housing, medical, and higher education prices cemented the view that the Reagan-Clinton run had solved some, but not all, of the problems of the stagflation era and had perhaps introduced new ones.

In recounting the history of the Reagan and Clinton years, it is useful to note that reform proceeded across the board, except in monetary affairs. In the realm of fiscal policy, tax rates tumbled, spending followed, and the federal budget went into a gaping deficit but then a surplus. Deregulation expanded, and free trade agreements burgeoned. On the monetary side, in contrast, there was only tinkering: occasional efforts to rein in exchange-rate swings with no serious consideration of reinstituting the gold standard.

When the legacy of the Reagan-Clinton run gave way, in the early 2000s, to smaller economic performance, to more clipped economic growth, as inflation kept to its circa 2–3 percent level, the public's dissatisfaction became clear soon enough. When the financial crisis began in the latter half of 2008, immediately came Bitcoin. If authorities were going to be satisfied with fiat money and not minister to classical monetary reform, innovations from the private sector would step in at the first whisper of crisis to do the job themselves.

The suppression of the monetary
issue in the 1980s and 1990s

Stagflation ended definitively at the beginning of 1983. In the latter half of 1982, inflation fell to the low levels that would hold for the next several decades. This marked the end of one half of stagflation. As for stagnation, it bit the dust several months later. Over 1983 and 1984, the American economy grew prodigiously, over 6 percent per annum, as price increases stayed low. The stock market response was seismic. The major indexes appreciated by 30 percent from mid-August through the end of the year 1982, only to reach higher and higher, indeed up over a dozen-fold, with some interruptions, over the next eighteen years.

The headline government policy, that of the Reagan administration that accompanied this transition, was a set of major reductions in the progressive tax-rate structure. On January 1, 1982, the top rate of the income tax fell from 70 to 50 percent and the top capital gains rate from 28 to 20 percent (having been effectively 49 percent in 1978). On January 1, 1983, cuts in rates below these top rates, which pending legislation in 1982 had threatened, came through. In 1988, the income tax was compressed to merely two rates, 28 percent at the top and 15 percent at the bottom. In 1963, in contrast, the top rate had been 91 percent and the bottom 20 percent, with many others in between. Higher tax rates mean that money takes longer to make, and therefore one loses a greater share of one's finite time in life.

Tax rates went way down in the 1980s. This spurred growth and production and a greater ratio of goods to money. Reagan's tax-rate cuts made stagflation impossible, and it ended.

The next unambiguously implemented economic policy of the Reagan administration concerned regulation. Reagan continued to fulfill the aggressive deregulation agenda of the preceding Jimmy Carter administration. President Carter had begun comprehensive deregulation of the trucking and airline industries. Reagan completed these endeavors and added further deregulation in major industries, including telephones. Concerning international trade, Reagan introduced quotas and other trade restrictions as the dollar appreciated sharply in the foreign exchange markets over the first half of the 1980s. His long-term policy was in the other direction, toward a North American free-trade zone and a more powerful global trading body smoothing the way for trade. Both of these came into being in the 1990s via the North American Free Trade Agreement (NAFTA) of 1994 and the World Trade Organization.

Reagan strove to cut domestic discretionary government spending and increased, sharply, military spending. His stated ideal of a distinctly smaller government, on the measurement of total spending, achieved realization in the 1990s, as federal outlays reached lows, as a percentage of the economy, previously seen in the 1960s. The Clinton administration of the 1990s maintained the outlines of all of Reagan's economic policies as its own major initiatives. The apparent departure of Clinton from Reagan concerned the top income tax rate. He took it up to 39.6 percent. However, even this was a compromise in Reagan's direction. The two Reagan tax cuts lowered the top rate from 70 percent first to 50 and then 28 percent. Clinton's top rate was the average of the two Reagan tax cut rates.

The roster of major presidential economic policies during the distinctly strong, disinflationary economic expansions of the 1980s and 1990s included *de jure* reforms in taxation, regulation, trade, and spending. In the area of monetary policy and the monetary regime, nothing comparable happened in *de jure* terms. There was no major initiative in the area of monetary affairs.

At times, monetary and exchange rate issues were the focus of attention and priority. But the cast of the activity was different from that of the other domains. Nothing of substance was ever legislated or otherwise made permanent in the spirit of reform. The Federal Reserve Chair Paul Volcker "shock" of the early 1980s referred to the unprecedentedly high interest rates of the early 1980s (prime at 21 percent, for example). The Federal Reserve was unquestionably active in especially the early 1980s and conspicuously striving to take clear and bold steps to dispatch the Great Inflation still operative as of early 1982. Yet it is unclear how tenable it is to maintain that the Federal Reserve can control a market interest rate. The legacy of a dozen-year mega-inflation was incredulousness on the part of the providers of credit. After such an experience, they needed no less than a healthy interest rate should they part with their money for coupon payments and a promise of a principal payment in nominal currency in the future. Economics had long taught that enduring, serious inflations erode the foundations of the interest rate base and require that interest rates go up and up until the inflation passes from the scene definitively.

This happened at last in 1983. Correspondingly, interest rates staggered down. That the Federal Reserve was busy the whole while, perhaps even professing to shock inflation into quiescence, may not be terribly relevant. The high interest rates of the early 1980s perhaps reflected little more than market awareness that inflation had been proceeding at stagflation levels for more than a decade, whatever the policy of the Fed. Moreover, there were ample alternative sources of the money supply that were outside the control of the Federal Reserve. Chief among these were the enormous global dollar accounts that had been getting ever larger ever since the switch to exchange rate flexibility in the early 1970s. When investments in the United States suddenly became attractive in the United States after 1982, immeasurable sums of foreign capital bounded into the United States to finance the expansion and stake a claim on the profits.

This also happened domestically. Those who had tried to best inflation by holding dollar-depreciation hedges, from gold to oil to land to collectibles, shifted out of these assets after 1982 and into American financial paper. It was another enhancement of the domestic money supply. It is important to go over such points in view of the aura surrounding the "Volcker shock" and the transition from the final stagflation-recession, that of the early 1980s, into the 1980s/1990s booms. The Fed may have well been a sideshow, as the vast global economic agents who really were the ones in control of the money supply withheld their resources first during the stagflation of the 1970s through 1980, and then as the Reagan plan struggled with implementation in 1981–82, only to be definitively in place by early 1983. Whatever may be said about the Reagan plan, it was not monetary. Its focus was on explicit reform in other domains—taxation, regulation, spending, and trade.

After the disinflationary boom started to run its course in the mid-1980s, the pertinent authorities shifted their attention from the conduct of monetary policy to the exchange rate. The dollar went up mightily against most currencies from 1981 to 1985. The United States engaged in shuttle diplomacy to provide functional foreign exchange bands for the dollar. A meeting at the Plaza Hotel in New York in 1985 strove to establish a ceiling for the dollar's value against foreign exchange. A 1987 meeting at the Louvre Museum in Paris strove to establish a floor. The bands were wide, at least ten times the 1-percent preferences of Bretton Woods. The policy that resulted from this diplomacy was not new laws, treaties, or official conventions, but pledges in the form of communiques. Countries including the United States would cooperate in keeping the dollar somewhat stable against other currencies.

Communiques, the Plaza, the Louvre—what did these fancy activities mean? Currency was still going to be fiat, undefined in gold or anything else, officially. The fixed-exchange-rate band commitment was not binding. Meanwhile, the United States was making shocking changes to its fiscal profile. The top personal income tax rate went from 70 to 50 to 28, and the top corporate rate from 48 to 46 to 34 percent. If other countries did not match these changes, up would go the dollar against foreign exchange as global money seeking better after-tax returns came in, no matter the communique. When in the late 1980s, Prime Minister Margaret Thatcher, after she engineered a tax-rate cut at the top in the United Kingdom, fixed the pound sterling to the West German mark, so much capital plowed into the country that British consumer price inflation hit double digits.

All the other domains—taxes, regulation, spending, trade— experienced explicit legal adjustment in the United States. Tax rates went down by statute. The regulatory and spending changes were by statute. Congress ratified NAFTA. Monetary affairs remained a realm of discretion, feel, and diplomatic exhibitionism. The signal attempt to reassert definition came in 1981–82, under a Congressional Gold Commission. Its majority advised against a gold standard, its minority in favor. The issue fell away in terms of official priority as the post-1982 boom got underway.

The price of gold in the private markets, for its part, fell from absurd levels beyond $800 and stayed within a band. For the fifteen years to 2000, gold stayed relatively stable at around $350 per ounce, ten times the official price from which Nixon had departed in August 1971. (Bitcoin, when falling by 50 percent, has often stayed in a narrow trading range afterward.) A sort of *de facto* gold standard operated regarding the dollar.

As soon as gold ticked up past $350, global suppliers of dollar credit pulled back. As gold fell below $350, these same suppliers, inclusive perhaps of the Fed, upped their allowances of loans and credits.

The ability of the markets to stabilize the dollar against gold, in the context of robust economic growth in the 1980s and 1990s, was enough to retire the matter of monetary reform in the direction of the pre-1971 order, at least on the part of officials and the scholarly and policy establishment. President Clinton's monetary activities were of a piece with Reagan's—an emphasis on Federal Reserve professionalism and a strong dollar. The departure from stagflation had not required, it appeared, any formal reform of the monetary system.

Discordant notes included the crushing increase in currency trading. Per annum growth rates of 10 percent, making this market the largest in the world in the 2000s, proceeded apace in the 1980s and 1990s. Furthermore, the unremitting expansion of world trade enabled greater amassing of exchange reserves. These were indications that after stagflation, monetary reform required seriousness of attention.

In grossly disproportionate terms, the financial sector expanded. Conventional estimates have banks, brokerages, credit agencies, financial advisors, and so forth accounting for, by the 2010s, double or triple the circa 3 percent of GDP in the United States prior to 1971. This sharp growth came at the expense of other sectors of the economy. When questions about the advisability of fiat money become closed at the official level, industry ministered to the quandaries unique to non-classical money systems by shifting enormous resources toward the profits to be made in the trading of currencies. The rest of the economy was the loser. One way of measuring, generally, the cost of going off gold was the share of GDP that finance took from the rest of the economy. Non-financial GDP share went down by at least 5 percentage points. This is a massive, trillion-dollar-plus yearly cost, the one the American economy endured on going off gold in 1971.

The mediocre 2000s

The huge bull market in stocks ending in 2000 lifted the new mass participatory device of the retirement account, the 401(k). Such financial devices had not existed before the late 1970s. The rise of the culture of saving for retirement came from a number of sources, to be sure. The decline of jobs-for-life and large firms with pension plans were one cause. Another was the entrenchment of secular inflation. The circa 3-percent long-term inflation rate of the post-1982 era compared to a 1-percent rate prior to 1965 and a nil rate prior to 1913. Moreover, investment gains are taxable. The hurdle rate for retirement savings, after taxes and inflation, was 4–5 percent per annum for most 401(k) savers. This required investments in aggressive asset classes, namely stocks, pushing people outward on the risk curve. The stock market greatly returned over the hurdle rate from 1982 to 2000. From 2000 to the present, however, it is not clear that it has. From 2000 to 2021, nearly the space of a generation, gold outperformed the Dow Jones Industrial Average.

The transaction costs of a suddenly enormous financial planning industry ministering to mass individually directed retirement accounts add another level, perhaps a full percent, to the hurdle rate. If the hurdle rate to make any money at all, in real after-tax, after-cost terms in stocks in the long term, is 6 percent, which it may be, there are few examples in stock market history (aside from 1982–2000) of gains comfortably above of that rate. The big rise in retirement planning aims, therefore, at the goal of saving money. Someone putting away money in a 401(k) will likely get years later in real, after-tax, after-fee terms what the money was worth originally. Perhaps because business managers are not enamored of mass retirement savings making up the capital markets, whose intelligent signals are essential to business guidance, private equity continues to displace publicly traded companies in terms of market and profit shares. Therefore, the era of even making 6 percent long term in stocks may be passing. If private equity continues its march, retirement accounts could become losing propositions.

In eras of classically defined money, saving was a simpler proposition. One saved it. A passbook savings account, a safe deposit box holding coin, a jar above the kitchen sink with bank notes and precious metals (guns at the ready on a rack), if perhaps the odd stock or bond as well, sufficed. There were security and failure problems in the old days, to be sure. Those costs would have had to reach 1 percent per annum to compete with the transaction costs of a latter-day retirement account; more than that to compete with the volatility risk in the stock market; and still more to deal with the depreciation risk of the currency and prospective levels of future taxation. Saving money has become a consuming matter requiring a lifetime of attention, professional services, employer matching, strategy, and planning. Such things are proper to ambitious businesses, perhaps, but to the ordinary members of a democratic populace who would prefer that their earnings and assets stay whole? What a clever method of appropriation from the common people.

Inherent in the architecture of the Great Moderation economy were foundational elements, such as retirement accounts and the explosion of the financial industry, that to some notable degree represented acquiescence to, a peacemaking with, fiat money. Yet it is not clear that major segments of the democratic population wanted a peacemaking with fiat money. Should not a monetary system worthy as a successor to the gold standard have been made a chief matter of policy and official priority after the difficulties of stagflation passed? Federal Reserve management of details and treasury-ministry shuttle diplomacy were about all anyone longing for monetary reform ever got.

A popular unease brewed beneath the economic wonders of the 1980s and 1990s. When the 2000s began inauspiciously, economically, and then failed to deliver a good recovery, the problems came to the surface. The President George W. Bush tax cut and spending policy was different from Reagan's. Bush's tax-rate cuts were thicker at the bottom than the top and set to expire after the not very long term of ten years. Domestic and military spending went up. And in a complete departure from the precedent of the Reagan and Clinton eras, the dollar depreciated badly against its old definitional asset, gold. At levels under $300 per ounce in the markets to begin the millennium, gold during W. Bush started shooting past the old thresholds, to $500 and then $1,000 and above. From 2000 to 2021, gold increased about sixfold; the Dow Jones industrials increased just over threefold.

In Jude Wanniski's classical formula, the signal was that global providers of money and credit were not satisfied with the investment environment in the transactions area of the United States dollar. Gold going up means that too much money is available, given realistic investment projects. The correction would be to see to it that the investment environment improves, calling money out of gold and into that environment. Government spending on domestic programs, let alone the Middle Eastern wars, plus tax rates set to go up after a few years, restricted the range and aspirations of the private economy in the United States, the domain of dollar-denominated capital investment. Gold substitutes, established as such in the inflation-hedge era of the 1970s, went up as well. Most notable was the medium by which the average person makes a play in land: housing. The Case-Shiller home-price index zoomed up 85 percent from 2000 to 2006.

Consumer price inflation in the early 2000s stayed at the post-stagflation norms. Not so the other indicators of dollar stability, such as the dollar's price against gold and gold alternatives, including beyond housing oil. The dollar struggled against foreign exchange as well. The euro appreciated 85 percent against the dollar from 2002 to 2008. Here were economies, the United States and the eurozone, that had similar growth rates, whose size was about the same, and that had an intimate trading relationship. How could there be mammoth changes in the respective values of their currencies? A cause of the great crisis of 2008 surely was, in part, the growing sense that it was impossible to make good investments in a world whose media of exchange gyrated wildly against each other.

The attention toward dollar policy, from the outset of the Great Moderation, had alternatively been showy and emphasized professionalism. Attention of this type warded off searching popular questions about the kind of monetary regime a great mature economy should have after it cashiered the gold standard. By the mid-2000s, the risks of the official posture began to show. Obviously, the dollar cannot fall against classical dollar hedges across the board without there being an investment and therefore a jobs crisis in the offing. As indeed, there was—the Great Recession of 2008–09.

The 1970s mocked the departure from gold and fixed rates savagely with stagflation. The Great Moderation had serious real accomplishments: the jobs boom, stock gains, and a burst in entrepreneurialism. Yet it also forced the population to deal with the rise of finance (and health care as well) at the expense of the other normal components of the economy, not least manufacturing. If there was a residual interest in returning to "sound money," as the nostalgia for gold and fixed rates formulated it, not only was the official answer no, but one also had to reorient life activities around financial plans and working on becoming a member of the "investor class." Robert Kiyosaki, author of *Rich Dad Poor Dad* (1997), has raised concerns about the mass retirement vehicles. Useful criticism of 401(k)s is that they can amount to the equivalent of savings accounts, complicated and restricted ones with high fees. Kiyosaki has proposed that that aspiring to achieve affluence in a fiat-money world has meant being a real investor in income-generating risk projects, perhaps in which one is personally involved, as opposed to being a hopeful 401(k) padder. Yet if money is no longer based on gold, even regular savers have to chase returns.

The Great Recession and a new dawn: The Bitcoin era

The symmetry was beautiful. As the economy fell into the Great Recession in the autumn of 2008, with stocks and banks collapsing, Bernard Madoff being exposed for naked swimming, and unemployment looming, out of nowhere that Halloween popped out the Bitcoin white paper. The author was "Satoshi

Nakamoto," whoever that may be. The formal purpose of the white paper was to propose a solution to a narrow, if significant, financial problem. The first words of the abstract: "A purely peer-to-peer version of electronic cash would allow online payments to be sent directly from one party to another without going through a financial institution." Bitcoin, the nine pages of this white paper proposed, could enable persons making transactions for things with money not to have to have that transaction settled by someone else.[48]

This was the nature of the cash economy for time immemorial. In 1850 America, a pile of silver coins for a sheaf of wheat: no third party, just buyer and seller. Even if the persons in question used private bank notes, which is to say paper dollars, as was common, there was no third party. Person A gives the dollars to person B, who takes the dollars and gives the wheat to person A. The transaction clears.

The other way is to have someone else pay person B on person A's behalf. Person A pays with a debit card, and person B gets an all-clear from the machine saying the issuer of the debit card is good for the amount of money in the account held by person A at the issuer's institution. Then, the issuer gives the money to another institution, where person B has an account. This was the third-party thickness that the Bitcoin white paper sought to eliminate as its central purpose.

To be sure, there are costs to having transactional third parties. The rate of interest (if any) on the accounts people maintain to make or get payments in cards and checks is lower than that rate would be if the institution did not have third-party transactions clearing expenses. These expenses amount to

---

[48] Satoshi Nakamoto, "Bitcoin: A Peer-to-Peer Electronic Cash System," at bitcoin.org/bitcoin.pdf, 1.

a minimum of 1 percent of cash balances, or a portion of the spread between cash and time-deposit interest. A peer-to-peer transaction system such as on the Bitcoin blockchain would restore the nil costs of the cash economy of yore.

The Bitcoin white paper used the terms "chain" and "block," if not "blockchain" itself. Every time Bitcoin changes hands on the computer network, the event necessarily has a time-stamp globally visible. "Each timestamp includes the previous timestamp in its hash, forming a chain, with each additional timestamp reinforcing the ones before it," went the white paper. That a transaction has taken place is a matter of inescapably clear public record. "The public can see that someone is sending an amount to someone else, but without information linking the transaction to anyone. This is similar to the level of information released by stock exchanges, where the time and size of individual trades, the 'tape,' is made public, but without telling who the parties were."[49]

Brilliant commentators such as Saifedean Ammous, in works such as *The Bitcoin Standard* (2018), have detailed the technological and financial advantages of Bitcoin. Ammous supremely, along with others, has assessed the criticisms leveled at Bitcoin. These include the natural resource use associated with blockchain-building, the chain's susceptibility to military and asymmetric attacks, threats from quantum computing, government marking of discrete Bitcoins, and criminal interest in cryptocurrency. In these pages, we stress the historical, political-economic, and social-psychological relevance of the emergence of Bitcoin.

---

[49]   Nakamoto, "Bitcoin," 2, 6.

Bitcoin came about after a long generation of free-form experimentation in fiat money that has no precedent in American history, if not the history of the world. Of the now five decades of that history since 1971, two of them, the 1980s and 1990s, were acceptable in terms of economic results. Three of them, including, along with the 1970s, the greater part of the 2000s, were unacceptable. All the while since 1971, transformations, any number of them dubious, overcame the economy as it adjusted to non-gold, non-defined money.

The 1970s were the first decade of pure fiat money and were unacceptable to a fault. There was the occasionally passable growth spurt in those weird years. Nevertheless, all the while, inflation eroded fixed income and banked money. Cost-of-living raises faced progressive tax rates, while investments had tax liability on gains that reflected consumer price increases. The election of 1980, which brought Reagan, marked *finis* to the indulgence of going off gold in 1971.

Reagan did not go back on gold—how odd—but gold still fell and stayed low. Bounding down from $800, it was about $300–$400 for the duration through 2000 after Reagan got his way legislatively with tax cuts after 1982. There were plenty of layoffs in the Reagan era, but thirty-eight million net new jobs materialized from 1980 to 2000. The Reagan plan forced corporate reorganizations, incurring layoffs, while the preponderant dynamic sectors of the economy added far more jobs than were lost. The 1980s and 1990s, on net, were fully acceptable by the high criteria of the American Dream. If people wanted remunerative work or opportunity, it was there to be had. Still, since there was no monetary reform back toward gold, inflation stayed at 2–3 percent per year, above historical norms by double at least. People piled into stocks, 401(k)s, and houses to hedge inflation and taxes. They did well because tax rates and government spending went down, regulation abated, and trade swelled. This gave ample room for the private economy—the domain of stocks—to roam.

One down decade, the 1970s, followed by two up decades, the 1980s and 1990s, inclusive of their indifference toward returning to gold money. Then came another down decade, the 2000s. The recession of 2000–01 gave way to a recovery of 2–3 percent in GDP growth, where 5–6 percent, if not 6–7 percent (the record of 1983–84), had been normal before. The gold market reacted accordingly. Mediocre growth out of recession meant hedging the monetary system. Gold tripled from 2000 to 2008. Global capital piling into gold means that it is not dedicated to private employment projects, which is to say real businesses. The Great Recession put the 1980s and 1990s to pasture. Officials forgot about monetary reform and gold, and eventually there was an economic crisis.

Private creativity, by giving us Bitcoin in 2008, began a new era. This first cryptocurrency is an instrument for recapturing the historical monetary system, the very one that gave us the Industrial Revolution. This was a system in which money had a final definition irrespective of the whim of the issuer. An ounce of silver, a twentieth of gold—unchangeable essences such as an ounce of something had been the definition of currency when the economy was prodigious in its output and extension of prosperity.

Bitcoin's history in the 2010s was one of price discovery. Was there really interest in such a device? From negligible values in the several years after 2008, it popped up over a dollar, and then even $1,000 in 2013. It settled in the $400 range in 2015–16, zoomed up to nearly $20,000 in 2017, and settled back at three-quarters of that level, before going up and down and up again over 2021–23. Eventually, as Bitcoin ownership extends to more individuals and institutions, its price may stabilize, presumably at some high level. When it does stabilize, among a wide ownership base, it can become part of the basis of a neo-classical monetary system.

The public once demanded that fiat currency have definition in gold or silver. It was so broadly understood that currency issuers defined their monies in such a fashion without much thinking about it. Classical monetary definition became a thing of the past in 1971, at the hands of officials. The public was not so sure. After decades of witnessing the pure fiat regime, an emulator of gold and precious metals emerged in Bitcoin under the auspices of the computer science revolution. Defining the dollar as a unit of gold or a proportionately larger unit of silver used to be a matter of course. The economic results of such a convention were the greatest in history. Officials deride gold in particular as irrelevant to the contemporary monetary system. The Bitcoin cult disagrees and is working to force the issue.

The World Ahead

The purpose of the preceding chapters has been to bring to light essential aspects of the history of money, especially as pertains to the United States. Two points are central. The first is that for the great majority of not merely history, but modern history, currency has had definitions to which currency issuers have submitted. The second is that currency issuers have normally been all sorts of agents, private and governmental alike, the preponderant number private.

We find the Bitcoin and cryptocurrency phenomenon of recent years to build on this history, indeed to recollect it and bid us to return to it in proper contemporary fashion. Bitcoin and crypto have reintroduced the concept, dormant for years, of the democratization of currency issuance. Anyone can issue a crypto, like just about anyone could issue a dollar in the old days. Moreover, Bitcoin in particular has strong characteristics of being final, definitional money. It, like gold, is limited in absolute stock; it is increasingly more difficult to obtain; its nature is independent and not a function of the currency issuer's wishes; it is clunky to use; and crucially, it has cult-like appeal in society.

Bitcoin is inviting us to relearn the great monetary history of the modern world, certainly of the United States—and on the basis of that relearning, figure out how to reinstitute the best aspects of our monetary system that went by the boards with the unprecedented move toward pure fiat money since 1971. An economic system with many suppliers is, in nearly every case, more efficient than one with a solitary supplier. The suppliers compete against each other to the benefit of the product and the consumer. When it comes to the product of money, we have lacked the advantage of competitive suppliers because governments and official central banks have arrogated, through force of law and regulation, the prerogative of supply to themselves. Bitcoin heralds a proper return to a system of competitive suppliers of money and currency.

Perhaps the most crucial point is that money is to have a definition. This was perfectly obvious in the United States for nearly two centuries. The "dollar" should have a definition in something that the country does not at all control, such as the elemental properties of gold or silver, materials that have proven that they can store the value of productive human time. If there is one facet of history that this book strives to emphasize above all, it is this. The dollar, for years, in the eighteenth, nineteenth, and a good part of the twentieth centuries, had an explicit defi-nition in something else—gold or silver. Moreover, the United States made this definition available for ultimately anyone to take advantage of. If somebody wants to issue a dollar, here is what it is, Congress said: one-twentieth of an ounce of gold, or an ounce of silver. Even when the United States issued its own currency under this definition, it had to compete against private issuers calling on the same definition. All these competitive currencies going against each other under a common definition went by the same name: the United States dollar.

The world of this system was no slouch. It was the world of the great Industrial Revolution. This is the kicker. When the United States, in particular, defined its currency in gold or silver and permitted competitive issuers of that currency, the dollar, the country soared to the greatest heights ever seen in economic history. The fantastic growth of the American economy in its heroic period occurred under the auspices of the kind of monetary system that we have forsaken. The immense growth of the nineteenth century, the high standard of living the immigrant masses bid for at the turn of the twentieth century, and the booms of the Roaring 1920s and post-World War II period, and despite the Great Depression of the 1930s, all occurred with a definitional United States dollar.

It is only since 1971 that anxiety has developed about owning houses, about finance replacing industry and agriculture as occupations, about whether the current generation has any hope of being as prosperous as the last. The post-1971, non-gold economy has only been passable when phenomenal tax and spending cuts, those of the 1980s and 1990s, ruled the day. Otherwise, the post-1971 non-gold economy has been mediocre at best. In one important sense, the post-1971 non-gold economy is worse than all other epochs of American economic history. Never before, as since 2000, has economic growth come in as low as sub-2 percent for decades on end.

In the next generation, there are three probable outcomes for the American (and world) monetary system. The first is the continuance of the status quo of king dollar dominating as the world's reserve currency. The second is the capitulation of king dollar and its ruin. The last is a fusion model—a middle or compromise scenario of a new independent anchor system that retains useful aspects of the current system.

For the dollar to persist in dominance, the satisfactoriness of the American economy will have to remain beyond question domestically and globally. This was not the case, for example, in the stagflation years of the 1970s and early 1980s. The inflation raging when Reagan took office stopped short, giving way to king dollar, as the monetary authorities (Paul Volcker at the Federal Reserve above all) were content to see interest rates float up very high, higher even than the extreme inflation rate. Inflation had been a false boon to governments. In the 1960s and 1970s, state and local governments (let alone Washington, DC) were able to expand rapidly due to inflation, in that their tax systems taxed nominal sales, income, and property values. Likewise, over the past twenty years, state and municipal debt, along with other obligations such as pensions, stayed high. But as real tax rates increase, people come to sour on the economy and decline to invest or even engage in economic activity very much (witness the Rust Belt). No economy in which its participants are not all that energetic about the affairs of business and enterprise will have a dominant currency.

Two primary factors drive the demand for a currency. One, inevitably, is the policy posture of the authorities, the Federal Reserve in the United States, as much in its regulatory as in its express monetary policy. The other, surely more important, is the assessment of those who own credit about the real prospects of those who desire it. Put more conventionally, in the supply and demand of the market, capital seeks the highest plausible return. Governments that have debt outstanding, current debt needs, and plans for future debt behold this reality with trepidation. Governments hooked on debt have a superficial conflict of interest with rapid economic growth, because such growth can push capital toward the private sector. Wise governments see that cutting tax rates in such beautiful contexts invariably brings Laffer curve effects and will sustain current debt payments as well as decrease the need for debt in the future.

Wise governments—a contradiction in terms? If interest rates sought their natural level today, budgetary catastrophe would appear to be the necessary result. Some $1 trillion is the (variable-rate) interest on the federal debt of $30 trillion-plus. State and local debt is $3 trillion. If interest rates moved to 10 percent or redoubled from there to 20 percent, many government entities would become insolvent. Perhaps voters will be pleased with half of the budget dedicated to interest payments, given that this should restrict the government's wherewithal for meddling in the economy. A Volcker 2.0 of letting raising rates go up high to bring back a strong, stable dollar is unlikely. The result may come anyway.

The strange status quo of the President Barack Obama years and beyond, of interest rates that were objectively low, either minuscule in number, near the zero bound as under Obama, or below the inflation rate as under President Joseph Biden, surely proved unsustainable. For free-marketeers, low interest rates ordinarily should signal that an economy is excellent—that anyone the world over will lend that economy money since its prospects are so great. Yet low rates also can reflect the regrettable efforts of authorities to continue in poor governance and to secure the capture of the banking sector with the lure of favorable regulation and bailouts (all this tantamount to corruption).

Beginning in 2008, the authorities kept buying certain financial assets whose owners they preferred to be the subject of bailouts. The buying continued far above the market-clearing price. The Federal Reserve balance sheet ballooned from the hundreds of billions to the many trillions. This is what happens when a willful authority does not care about price but about saving those asset-holders that the authority prefers, compromising the price signals of the unit of account (in this case, the dollar) worldwide. Post-2008, the Great Recession mustered a long, poor recovery because the market for bad assets had a big fool buyer. If the status quo were suddenly reformed, it would be painful for the bureaucracy, because the jobs and sweetheart deals within and enabled by the bureaucracy, including in the private financial sector, would become irrelevant. Currently the incentives are not aligned to induce reforms. Yet if reform does not occur, one of the other two probable outcomes proposed above will come to the fore.

The capitulation and ruin of king dollar would be a bigger event than Nixon's closing of the gold window. It would alter the dynamics of the global economy and balance of power. Perhaps China could take over and dominate money, a real possibility, a real threat. Nonetheless, it would be difficult for China to decouple from the dollar. The Chinese currency is essentially backed by and defined in king dollar. The stable rate of exchange China has engineered for three decades now against the dollar means that the credibility of the Chinese currency comes from the dollar's credibility. Reinventing a national currency in a rapid transition is difficult, courting economic upheaval. This is a scenario for which many crypto enthusiasts admittedly cheer. There would be a fair chance that Bitcoin, or a rival cryptocurrency, could emerge as a powerful currency. This scenario should be considered seriously, not least so that we might ponder the ramifications. Events of this nature surely would not be linear, but follow according to a step function, a major one at that.

A fusion model with a new independent anchoring system would use new technological advances to support the value of government fiat currencies. Legal tender laws would have to be reformed for this to happen. New technologies and techniques for settling payments and making money would have to be free of legal tender and tax constraints. The fusion model would involve the anchoring techniques recently invented and pioneered and remain open to further advances in information technology innovation. Communications developments—blockchain technology, most prominently—offer fascinating solutions with regard to new money. Instead of the government creating money through central banks and their surrogates, private issuers would take risks. These efforts would replicate the benefits that bimetallism had in previous times. There is no bar to the dollar still being a dollar—only, under a fusion model, it would abide by a definition as in the past, and surely involving gold as well as Bitcoin. All government payments and debt could still be denominated in national currency. A fusion model moves past the fiat model of faith in government bankers to a system of trusting but verifying. This system would capitalize on the benefits of the current systems (such as the ease of moving capital around globally) while improving the store of value characteristic of money. It would permit a market demand for competitive currencies and let seigniorage occur, with a feedback loop controlling excesses. The drawback to such a system, at least from the perspective of governments and those who profit from government, is that it would constrain government spending and regulation.

How would a fusion model look? That is for the future to tell. Let us take a few guesses by using the wisdom of the past to peer up the trail in the quest for optimal money. Bitcoin is in the news often. It is sensational, in the attention-grabbing sense. The anchoring-Bitcoin advocates hold that the value of Bitcoin lies in its scarcity. As for those who quite reasonably say that Bitcoin sounds made up, it is worth noting that so is fiat money, which is all contemporary money. Scarcity can be an anchoring quality if it can represent time in a recognized stored manner, as gold has proven throughout the ages and other commodities (such as rare art) have at times as well.

"Hypothecation" is a banking term referring to what happens in fractional reserve banking when one dollar is lent out for twenty dollars or more worth of loans, in the old days the one dollar being the gold value stored at a bank. The hypothecation of Bitcoin has not yet been experimented with sufficiently for Bitcoin to be a replacement for base money. Such a development would reveal the capacity Bitcoin has for fulfilling the functions that money should fulfill. In the post-Bretton Woods era, one currency, the not-so-sound dollar, has been the medium of exchange and unit of account. So far, Bitcoin and crypto hypothecation has been essentially limited to scams or dubious yield-farming strategies concerning which executives are coy about where the yields are coming from.

For centuries, banks were able to hypothecate their reserve assets to conduct fractional banking activities. One theory as to why we have central banks is that the big banks tired of good, normal business and wanted a backstop to relieve them of being such diligent watchers of the economic scene. It must have been so very exhausting, all that concentrating and prudential judgment. Now, we have let the bankers' brains and sense of scrupulousness relax given bailouts. In a system in which money is anchored to a reserve asset, as we have emphasized repeatedly, there is an inherent feedback loop communicating to society—and to everyone on the spot, including bankers who have to suppress laziness and pay attention—when and where savings should be deployed. In a modern world in which people do not save (they either consume or are forced to speculate) and money does not store value, this feedback loop has given way, most unfortunately, to the poor substitute of government power, cronyism, and financial sector backstopping. With new block-chain technology paired with Bitcoin and perhaps other allied cryptocurrencies, a good gold dollar could make new digital money that could be used like gold was used in banking before. Back when, communication transmitted through telegraph to banks, and now, it would be on a blockchain—to the smart-phone instantly. People could send and make money with their independent freedom, and the feedback loop would rise again.

When the dollar abided by a definition, feedback loops worked throughout the monetary system to ensure the proper quantity and allocation of money and currency. If the public generally thought there was too much currency outstanding, increases in specie redemption requests quickly indicated it. Precious metal prices going down, in turn, revealed to currency issuers that the public demanded more of their monetary media for useful purposes. These feedback loops worked on the micro level as well. If an individual issuer saw special demand or redemption requests for its dollar, this was an indication of the probity of that issuer and the condition of its local economic environment.

The abandonment of dollar definition, on the cancellation of the gold standard in 1971, removed the basis of the feedback loops that had served the monetary system and the economy so well. When the Fed and its regulated banks issued the dollar and credit too much or too little, there was no message built-in at the point of issue about the problem. Therefore, the marketplace developed a host of substitutes. The private price of gold skyrocketed. By the 2020s, it was fifty times the thirty-five-dollar-per-ounce level it had been holding for decades prior to 1971. Finance gobbled up shares of GDP at the expense of ordinary production as owners of capital determined ways to hedge the dollar. Currency trading, land and house buying, and 401(k)s all boomed. At the best of times, inflation was 2–3 percent. In the 1970s and in 2022, it was much higher.

Not having the feedback loop of the gold standard expressed itself in the chronic depreciation of the currency. Complaints that the pre-Federal Reserve era saw bank and currency crises fail to reckon with how minor those crises were compared to the epic dollar depreciation that has come in the era of the Federal Reserve and the abrogation of the gold standard. Bad bank notes and bank busts in the nineteenth century might have summed to an annual loss of 1 or 2 percent of money outstanding, while the dollar held its value against goods and services. In the half-century since 1971, inflation of 1 or 2 percent for the long term would have been a cause for rejoicing.

Potential reckonings are building in the marketplace. The CEO of MicroStrategy, Michael Saylor, leveraged the profitable balance sheet of his initially modest company to acquire Bitcoin. As of the early 2024 price spike, MicroStrategy had 1 percent of the total Bitcoin that in the current community agreement will ever be. MicroStrategy continued to plow essentially all of its excess cash, plus credit it could get through favorable low corporate-customer interest rates, into buying more Bitcoin. As MicroStrategy's market capitalization got bigger and bigger, the company's stock grew large enough to be included in the major investment-vehicle indexes. Therefore, fund managers had to start buying MicroStrategy so that they owned every stock in the indexes. As Bitcoin increased in price, everyone had to buy this stock.

Other companies perceived what was going on and determined to make sure that they retained their share of investors' attention. Block (formerly Square) decided to use a share of its profits to acquire Bitcoin. Other major companies plotted to follow suit. As this process continues to unfold broadly, everyone with a retirement account will either directly or indirectly have exposure to the price of Bitcoin, because Bitcoin will come to be an asset item of a considerable portion of stocks within an index. This can trigger a cascade effect whereby nearly all companies, especially those with massive cash flows like Apple (Tesla already owns Bitcoin), buy Bitcoin. If it becomes common for trillion-dollar companies to acquire Bitcoin to protect and generate shareholder value, what then will the price of Bitcoin be, and who could afford to sit out? If the monetary system is going to switch toward a modern classical variety, given the arrival of Bitcoin, the implications for cash management of portfolios and corporate balance sheets are enormous.

Real banks print money on a common definition, but our banks transmit government money. If a real bank does a bad job, it fails, but modern banks get bailouts because they are an agent of the government. Representational money and a recovery of what banks actually were in history—their job was to make money on a common definition—regaining the sense of this reality is the opportunity that "distributed ledger technology," of all things, has brought to us today.

Bitcoin has emerged to remind us of what we lost by forsaking the gold standard and to give us an opportunity to reinvigorate that standard in contemporary terms. In particular, it offers a return to a new form of bimetallism. Perhaps in the future, when the price of Bitcoin stabilizes at a healthy, presumably quite high level, by virtue of mass ownership, a steady ratio between gold and Bitcoin will emerge. A dollar could be defined as a quantity of gold or the equivalent in Bitcoin. If the American authorities do not want to go this route (they could start by eliminating the capital gains tax on cryptocurrency transactions), the private sector will be able to take care of the matter. Another token or another fiat currency could define itself as such and provide competition to the undefined dollar. The ingredients for a fully prosperous twenty-first century are coming into being given Bitcoin's challenge to fiat money. A wise and generous society, one wishing to be good to itself, will take advantage of the opportunity. Let us free our money and flourish in tomorrow's freedom.

BIBLIOGRAPHIC NOTE AND ACKNOWLEDGMENTS

O ne of the central points of this book is that Americans used to discuss the details of money and dollar policy all the time, with direct and unapologetic consequences for policy. Grains of gold, bimetallic ratios, and much else consumed popular attention. Pamphlets flew on such subjects. People from all walks of life formed and expressed opinions about the money setup in the country. Elections turned on the issue. It was this way, perhaps, for economic matters in general. No economic mind, scholar or lay, has ever been as popular or widely read, quoted, and followed as the great, and most formally untutored, nineteenth-century economic philosopher Henry George.

Only with the rise of modern bureaucracies, including the Federal Reserve, has our politics and society sought to suppress monetary dialogue, to reserve proper commentary and influence on monetary matters to an expert elite comprising business and scholarly muckety-mucks. Somehow the Federal Reserve has become stacked with doctors of philosophy (PhDs) as well as agents and executives of the financial businesses who benefit from Fed backstopping. We feel that it is no accident that as this development, at once intellectually snobbish and economically insular (if not self-dealing), has taken hold, the integrity of money has disintegrated, and with it the consistent booming economic growth that had been the nation's birthright before. The Fed is a jobs program for the credentialed and connected, as money rots. In ages past, money policy was a central entry in robust, popular-democratic conversation and discourse.

In this book, we quote from numerous latter-day scholars of money who have informed the content of the history we offer, and we wish to recommend the work of each of these authors even beyond the pieces that we directly cite. Other important modern expositors of money whose work we have found instructive include George Gilder, Judy Shelton, Lawrence H. White, Peter Thiel, Steve Forbes, Elizabeth Ames, Lew Lehrman, Steve Hanke, Ron Paul, Larry Kudlow, John Tamny, Richard Salsman, Kevin Warsh, Robert Leeson, Roy Jastram, and (reaching further back in time) Carl Menger. Notwithstanding how instructive and inspiring each of these authors truly is, still we see the problem of scholarly commentators and inside players being the ones who talk, overtalk perhaps, about money. Perhaps in certain circles people overtalk about money because money remains not right—it is a real problem. (How PhDs are experts in money is not at all clear—generally, PhDs distinguish themselves, among the accomplished more broadly, as being the impecunious ones.) *Free Money* itself is a book, a treatise, a history, one coauthored by a financial practitioner (Benton Howser) and a scholar (Brian Domitrovic). We feel that Bitcoin is beckoning toward greater integration of popular, political, business, and scholarly exchange on monetary affairs—toward a maturation of the nation's intellectual discourse along with a maturation/restoration of a classical-like system.

We would like to thank those who have helped us in preparing this book in terms of its ideas and scope, including all those involved at the Philadelphia Society (which brought the coauthors together), Arthur Laffer and Nick Drinkwater at the Laffer Center, Cathie Wood, Jeanne and Rex Sinquefield, Dick Strong, Avik Roy, Steve Moore, Sharon Davis, Rod Roudi of Bitcoin Park, Paul Coleman, Justin Koscher, Mark Molesky, Paul Fortunato, Samantha Kowalchuk, Peter Kowalchuk, Tom Cox, Michael Carlisle of InkWell Management, and Madeline Sturgeon and Anthony Ziccardi of Post Hill Press.

ABOUT THE AUTHORS

Brian Domitrovic is the Richard S. Strong Scholar at the Laffer Center in Nashville. He is the author of six books, each on some facet of the history of supply-side economics, including, with Arthur Laffer and Jeanne Sinquefield, *Taxes Have Consequences: An Income Tax History of the United States* (2022). He holds a PhD in history from Harvard University. His website is www.globalmonetarism.com.

Benton Howser has been a high-frequency trader and registered investment advisor and is the founder of Atlas Veritas L.P., a registered hedge fund. He studied history at Virginia Tech, where he was a member of the Corps of Cadets, and earned a Master's of Business Administration from the University of Illinois at Urbana-Champaign. He currently serves as an Army Reserve Officer.